MAKE IT
YOUR
OWN

MAKE IT YOUR OWN

25 STYLISH PROJECTS FOR YOUR HOME

ANNA ALICIA

CONTENTS

INTRODUCTION

As a craftsperson I'm somewhat surprised to find myself writing a book, but this particular book brings together so many things so close to my heart that it feels at the same time serendipitous.

The joy of making things is inexpressible and utterly personal, so I'll leave you to discover or re-discover that through making some of the 25 projects I've designed for this book. I hope that my guidance, and Jacqui Melville's beautiful photographs, will inspire you to get your hands dirty, so to speak, but also to explore your own thoughts on design (whether that's something you're comfortable with already or something you're working out).

Similarly, the meanings attached to a place we call home are difficult to put into words and unique to each and every one of us, but what matters most to me in the idea of a home is the freedom to really make it an expression of yourself – a place that suits your practical and emotional needs. This doesn't have to mean knocking down walls and ripping up carpet, as I hope the projects here show. None of the projects take more than a day to make and some take under an hour, they use simple techniques, are all portable and most importantly adaptable to your own style/needs.

Also close to my heart is an engagement with materials, not only their seductive properties like colour, texture and weight, but also their provenance – how they are grown/made and by whom. I have compiled a list of suppliers at the back of this book (see page 142), focusing on eco-ethical and locally made materials/supplies.

My hope for this book is that it might lead to you making beautiful things that you will live with and treasure every day.

BY WAY OF A FURTHER INTRODUCTION TO ME AND MY WORK I ASKED MY GOOD FRIENDS AYESHA AND BRIAN TO ASK ME SOME QUESTIONS

As a child, what did you want to be when you grew up?
A marine biologist.

What was the first thing you ever made for your home?
The first thing I can remember making was an embroidered cushion with a concealed pocket for storing secret notes. I must have been about eight or nine and I think the inspiration came from something I'd seen on *Antiques Roadshow*! I was fascinated by the interplay between decoration and function in household objects, and the way their meanings often go beyond both, whether subversively (through secret pockets or coded embroidery) or through an emotional attachment or history (like crockery brought back from travels or passed down through the generations).

What's the best compliment you've ever received?
It sounds really soppy, but seeing someone buy, use or enjoy something I've made always feels like a huge compliment.

What's the most important lesson you've learnt so far?
I guess, so far, it would be that there aren't as many rules as I used to think there were! There isn't necessarily a right way to do something, just lots of different possibilities. I've taken a bit of a roundabout path to end up here, writing this book about making things, and sometimes I've seen that as a bad thing or even felt like a bit of a fraud. But, actually, I think that roundabout path has been essential to what I hope will make this book special. I'd like this book to be a guide (rather than any kind of rule book) for experimenting with design a little and making beautiful things that really make the place you live in feel like *your* home.

What's on your work desk at the moment?
The French-knitted necklace I was halfway through making when I stopped to get a cake and make some tea. Also, a wooden tray full of thread and pompom makers, old mugs of scissors and small tools, a tape measure, a collection of postcards from museums and, always close at hand, is a beautiful burgundy and yellow crocheted pincushion that I bought from another designer–maker (Namolio) several years ago – it's always full of multicoloured pearl-headed pins and an assortment of needles. Oh, and my reading glasses!

City or countryside ?

Though I am an absolute plant addict, I am completely in love with London and it feels like home, so it has to be the city. I still get to indulge in some very compact gardening even in the city – my little flat and its tiny balcony are overflowing with plants!

Tell us a secret about living in London, an undiscovered gem ?

Before I became a designer-maker I had no idea about all the amazing workshops and studios dotted around London. Many of them run open-studio events where you can nose around people's workspaces and buy directly from the makers (Craft Central and Cockpit Arts for instance). They're hugely inspiring.

What would you say to someone who has never made anything before but wants to try one of your projects ?

If I can make it, chances are you can too! Although I have been sewing for a very long time, I've never had any formal training in textiles, so there's nothing very technical here! My aim was to create simple projects with a focus on thinking about design and discovering your own style, rather than learning any tricky craft skills. The projects are all designed so that they can be easily adapted and developed (with suggestions in each one), so that when you're ready, you can explore putting your own design stamp on a project. It might take a bit of practise (maybe trying out some of the quicker projects first), but once you get going you may just fall in love with making things.

What's your motto to live your life by ?

Be generous. (I picked it up many years ago from an episode of *ER* when Dr Greene gave his daughter advice, but I don't think that matters!)

INSPIRATIONS

I'd need an entire extra chapter to talk about my inspirations properly – those I've been mulling over for years and the new ones I discover almost daily – but I've gathered together a few odds and ends from around my studio that I hope will give some insight into what's behind many of the projects in this book.

I have two distinct sides to my design interests: one is bright, folky and clashing, while the other is simple, clean and geometric. Some spaces in my own home lean more towards one than the other, but I always enjoy how these two elements can work together so I rarely feel the need to choose between them. For my home to be a real reflection of me, there needs to be both.

The little vintage purse in the picture is a great example of the stylized floral patterns and contrasting colours that have inspired several of the projects. Similarly, the gorgeous hand-woven fabric by a friend of mine, Sarah Lowry, has all the elegant geometric patterns and soothing colours I could ever want!

Materials are also a huge inspiration to me in and of themselves. Wanting to see the texture of wool against smooth cotton, or a richly coloured crossweave fabric against a pale one, are exactly the kinds of impulses that often spark my designs. I try as much as possible to let the materials speak for themselves, to let their texture, weight, colour or pattern be the foundation of a design.

I would hazard a guess that the colours I'm drawn to could be traced back primarily to flowers and paintings (especially Gauguin!) and a balancing of neutral or natural and vivid – like a bouquet of foliage and blooms.

Of course, what each person finds inspiring is a unique mix. The most important thing to remember is that no one style is right, and simply to be open to what that mix might be for you.

Clockwise from top left:
Vintage embroidery templates, vintage hand-embroidered purse, hand-woven fabric sample by Sarah Lowry, patterned ribbons and trim.

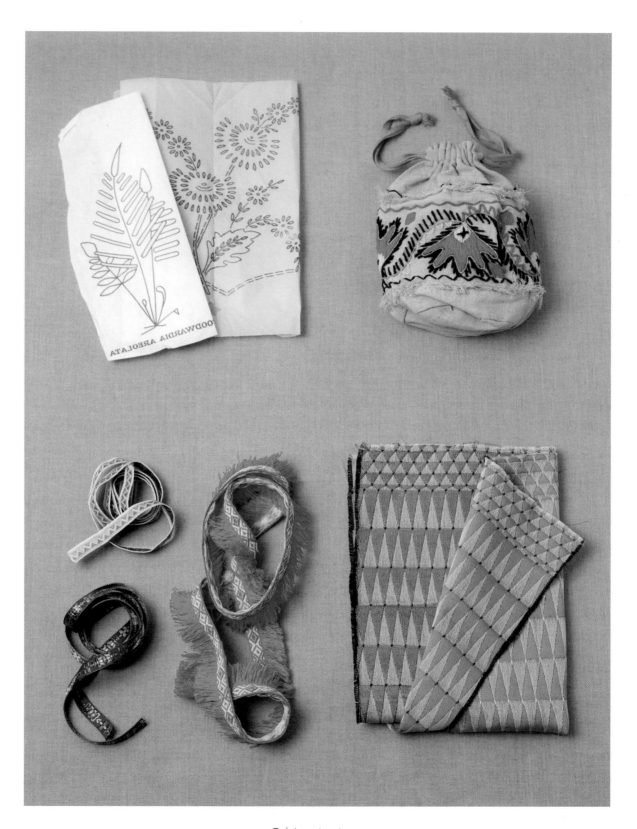

BASICS

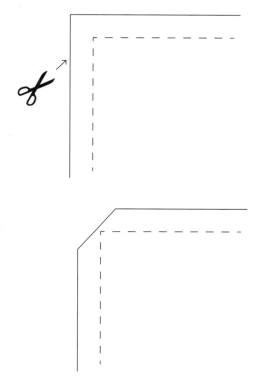

CORNERS

Several projects ask you to cut across the corners of your fabric after you've sewn it, so that you will have neater corners once your fabric is turned the right way round. Left is a little diagram of what I mean by that (cut about 2 mm [1/8 inch] from the corner of your stitching).

MACHINE SEWING

Unless otherwise specified, all machine sewing should be a standard straight stitch.

MATERIALS

I've mentioned the materials I've chosen to give you an idea of why I've picked particular colours, weights and textures, but feel free to experiment with whatever you have stashed away or what's catching your eye in the haberdashery department.

Some of the projects need a sturdy fabric for structure or durability, so just keep that in mind when choosing for those projects.

OUTLINES

Once marked out with tailor's chalk, some projects call for fabric to be cut along the outline exactly, while others are cut outside the chalk line to allow for a seam. Follow the cutting instructions project by project.

SUPPLIERS

I've included a list of suppliers on page 142 with a focus on Eco-ethical and locally made products, because shopping ethically is something close to my heart.

TEMPLATES

If you make templates for a project, it's worth labelling them and keeping them in a folder, as I find I often end up re-using them for similar projects.

ORGANISING

I'm not a naturally tidy person, this much I do know, so finding ways to organise, store and display stuff is essential! But that doesn't mean it needs to be about hiding things away. Most of the projects in this chapter are aimed at creating a place for objects – like the Machine-embroidered Eco-felt Baskets (see page 14) or the Pinboard projects (see pages 36 and 38). Your space can be both tidy(ish) and full of the things you use – and the things you just love too much to conceal. And, of course, there's no reason why the storage systems themselves (from the Champagne-cork pegs to the Cube Bookends, on pages 30 and 42) shouldn't be beautiful as well as practical!

Machine-embroidered Eco-felt Baskets

I absolutely love woven baskets, but basketry is a skill I'm yet to possess – it's on my list of things to learn! What I've tried to create here is a textile alternative. These baskets are lightweight and portable – ideal for storing the little things I use all the time, from thread in my studio to spare candles in my front room. Felt is the perfect material for this project: it's easy to sew but gives the baskets a firm enough structure so that they hold their shape.

MATERIALS AND EQUIPMENT

*The quantities given here are for one basket.
The colours you choose will really bring out
the detail, so be sure to use felt in contrasting
colours (with a brighter colour for the inside)
and use threads that will show up well against
your outer colour.*

M

– 2 sheets of eco-felt in contrasting colours,
 at least 23 cm x 23 cm (9 inches x 9 inches)
– Cotton thread in a range of colours
– Cotton thread to match your outer felt colour
– Cotton thread to match your inner felt colour

E

– Tailor's chalk
– Ruler
– Scissors
– Sewing machine
– Pins

HOW TO

1   Using your tailor's chalk, mark out a 23 cm (9 inch) square on each of your sheets of felt. (If you are making lots of baskets you may find it quicker to make a square template from a piece of card or paper and draw around this). Cut out your two squares along the chalk lines.

2   Thread your sewing machine with your first choice of coloured thread. Use the thread matching your outer felt colour for the bobbin (this means you won't have to change the bobbin thread each time you change the colour of your main thread).

3   Set your machine to a zigzag stitch (if your machine has a choice of zigzag sizes go for a medium or large one). Take the felt square you have chosen for your outer colour and sew a line of zigzag stitch across one end (it doesn't matter which end you start with), 1 cm (3/8 inch) from the edge (see diagram A).

4   Sew a second zigzag line in the same colour, 0.5 cm (1/4 inch) underneath the first line.

5   Repeat steps 3 and 4 along the opposite edge.

6   Now change to your next thread colour (you don't need to change the bobbin colour) and sew another line of zigzag stitch 0.5 cm (1/4 inch) underneath the second line. Do this on both edges.

7   Now change to your third colour and sew a line of zigzag 0.5 cm (1/4 inch) underneath the third line on both sides.

8   Continue in this way, sewing one or two lines in each colour until you have 6 or 7 lines in the same colour order along both edges (see diagram B).

9   Lay your square on a flat surface with the multicoloured stitching facing up. Fold your square in half so that the two edges with the stitching meet, and pin along the short sides (see diagram C).

10   Set your machine to a standard straight stitch and thread with the same coloured thread as your felt. Sew along the short sides, 1 cm (3/8 inch) from the edge, removing the pins as you go.

11   Now we need to square off the bottom corners to create the basket shape. (I was a bit daunted by squaring off corners when I first started sewing, as it looks a bit like some kind of complicated origami fold, but once you've done it once it'll seem like the

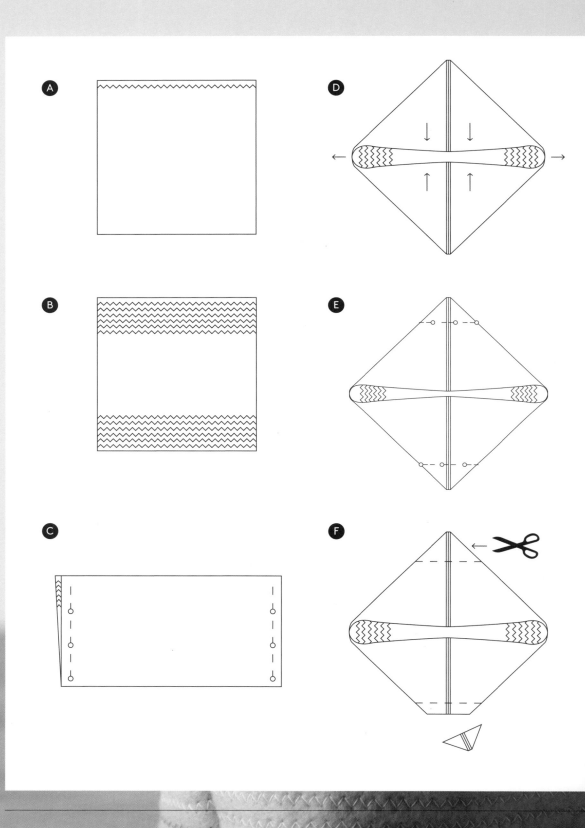

simplest thing on earth!) Hold your little felt 'envelope' in front of you with the open edge facing up and one of the seams pointing away from you. With both hands, place your thumbs inside and pull the two sides of the envelope away from each other. Allow the end seams to flatten down, keeping them central, so that they align with one another in a straight line and you end up with a triangle at each end (see diagram D).

12 From the tip of the triangle, measure 5 cm (2 inches) along one of your seams and mark this point with tailor's chalk. Then, using this mark as a guide, draw a line all the way across, at a right angle to the seam (I judge the right angle by eye, but you could use a set square if you'd like to be exact). Pin along this line (see diagram E).

13 Repeat this on the other seam, then sew along your pinned lines with a straight stitch, removing the pins as you go.

14 Cut your triangle corners away 1 cm (⅜ inch) from the lines you've just sewn (see diagram F).

15 Now turn your basket inside out, so that the seams are on the inside – the outside layer is complete!

16 For the inside layer of your basket, take your second square of felt and follow points 9 (it doesn't matter which edges meet as there's no embroidery) to 14, leaving the seams on the outside this time.

17 Now you're ready to put your two layers together. Sit your inner layer inside your outer layer and press into the corners, so that they fit neatly together and all the seams are between the two layers. Your inner layer will stick out a bit at the top but this is fine for now.

18 From the outside, pin the two layers together along the top edge.

19 Set your machine to the same zigzag stitch you used earlier. Thread your bobbin with thread the same colour as your inner layer, and use one of your other colours for the main thread.

20 Stitch your two layers together around the top edge of your outer layer, removing the pins as you go.

21 Trim any overlapping excess felt from the top of the inner layer close to the top of the outer layer, to give a neat edge. It's fine if the inner layer overlaps by a tiny bit – in fact, a little rim of the brighter colour showing over the top looks great!

MAKE IT YOUR OWN

- *I chose a simple design of zigzag rows for these baskets, inspired by the woven baskets I'd been admiring, but there are all sorts of other ways you could decorate yours. Depending what stitches your sewing machine can do, you could still go for rows but choose more elaborate stitches, or you could freestyle with your stitching and create all kinds of patterns or images.*

- *It's really easy to vary the size and shape of these baskets. Just play around with the size of the squares and how far you square off the corners to create baskets with different proportions.*

Carton
Doorstop

I wanted to use a simple, timeless design as the basis for this little household essential, so I ended up with a milk carton as inspiration!

MATERIALS AND EQUIPMENT

I ordered some gorgeous cerise pink organic cotton twill for this project, but when it arrived I completely fell in love with the back of the fabric (which, because of the way it's woven, has a fine diagonal white-and-cerise stripe), so I've actually used the reverse of the fabric as the front – and why not?!

M

- Cotton twill fabric (or any mid-weight fabric) at least 30 cm x 60 cm (12 inches x 24 inches)
- Cotton thread to match your fabric
- Approximately 3.5 kg (8 lb) dry rice or lentils

E

- Tailor's chalk
- Tape measure
- Scissors
- Pins
- Sewing machine
- Iron
- Needle

HOW TO

1. Using your tailor's chalk, mark out a rectangle of fabric 30 cm x 60 cm (12 inches x 24 inches). Cut it out along the chalk lines and lay out, right side up.

2. Fold the fabric rectangle in half so that the shorter edges meet at the top and pin together along the two sides (see diagram A). Sew along the two sides, 1 cm (⅜ inch) from the edge, removing the pins as you go. You'll end up with a 30 cm x 30 cm (12 inch x 12 inch) square.

3. Now we need to square off the bottom corners to create the cube shape. Hold the fabric 'envelope' you've sewn in front of you with the open edge facing up and one of the side seams pointing away from you. Pull the two sides of the envelope away from each other. Allow the seam that's facing away from you to flatten down towards you (see diagram B). You want to end up with a triangle pointing away from you and the seam running central.

4. From the tip of the triangle, measure 7 cm (2¾ inches) along your seam and mark this point with tailor's chalk. Then, using this mark as a guide, draw a line all the way across, at a right angle to the seam (I judge the right angle by eye, but you could use a set square if you'd like to be exact). Pin along this line (see diagram C).

5. Turn your fabric round and repeat this on the other corner, then sew along your pinned lines, removing the pins as you go. Now turn your fabric inside out (so that the seams are on the inside)

6. Fold in 2 cm (¾ inch) of fabric all the way around the top of your doorstop and press in place with an iron.

7. Stand up your fabric cube and pour in your rice or lentils until it is approximately two-thirds full.

8. Next we need to fold in the top to form the carton shape. Fold the top edges together as in diagrams D, E and F and pin in place. Make sure your top edges line up neatly.

9. Lastly, with a plain running stitch, hand sew your top edges together forming a rectangle, as in diagram G.

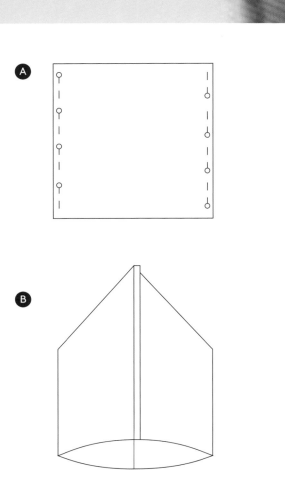

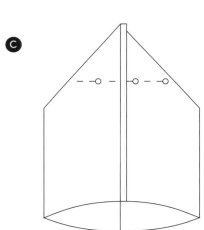

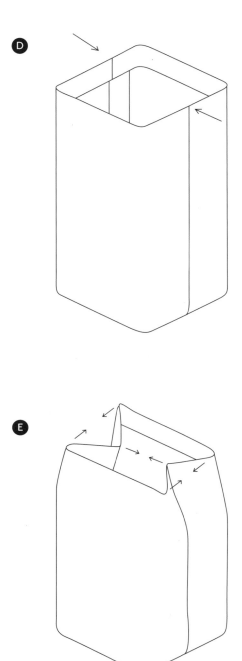

MAKE IT YOUR OWN

- *If you have a pretty fabric that you'd really like to use but it's not thick enough, you can simply layer this up with a plain, heavier fabric so your doorstop is good and sturdy.*

- *If, like me, you have balcony doors (on the windy seventh floor in my case!) you might want to scale up the design to make a slightly larger doorstop or fill it with something heavier, like sand.*

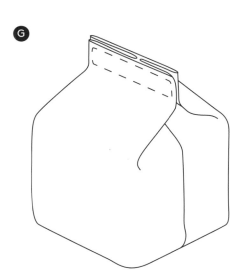

Carton Paperweight

There's definitely a place in my life for paperweights to keep things in nice, neat piles. Whether they're on my desk, with its endless mess of receipts, notes, business cards and various odd bits of paper, or the low shelf by our front door with its unruly pile of post. This one is a scaled-down version of the Carton Doorstop project (on page 20) and I love the idea of the big and little versions being used in the same room.

MATERIALS AND EQUIPMENT

M
- Cotton twill fabric (or any mid-weight fabric) at least 14 cm x 28 cm (5½ inches x 11 inches)
- Cotton thread to match your fabric
- Approximately 320 g (11 oz) dry rice or lentils

E
- Tailor's chalk
- Tape measure
- Scissors
- Pins
- Sewing machine
- Iron
- Needle

HOW TO

1   Use your tailor's chalk to mark out a rectangle of fabric 14 cm x 28 cm (5½ inches x 11 inches). Cut it out along the chalk lines and lay out, right side up.

2   Now follow steps 2 to 9 of the Carton Doorstop project on page 21, changing the measurement at step 4 to 3 cm (1¼ inches) and the measurement in step 6 to 1 cm (⅜ inch).

MAKE IT YOUR OWN

- If you have a home office or workspace, these would look great as a little set in different colours, keeping your paperwork firmly in place.

- I've kept this design really simple, but if you want to make more of a feature of your paperweight (or doorstop) you could experiment with embroidering, stencilling or even dip-dying the fabric before you make the project (you can find instructions for all these techniques throughout this book! See pages 54, 92 and 126).

Striped Clothes Pegs

As well as hanging up the washing, these little pops of joyous stripy colour can brighten up your life in a million and one ways! My favourite is to use them to display a collection of cards, photos, fabric or vintage handkerchiefs. Simply string up a piece of cord or ribbon, or gather a bundle of long, sturdy twigs in a jar or vase, and peg away!

MATERIALS AND EQUIPMENT

M
- Wooden clothes pegs (as many as you want to paint!)
- Acrylic paint in several colours
- Clear-drying craft glue (optional; see step 6)

E
- Narrow masking tape
- Small paintbrush

MAKE IT YOUR OWN

- *Stripes are, of course, optional. With a fine brush you can paint on any pattern you like, or just paint each peg in a single bold colour.*

- *These would make gorgeous place setting 'cards' for a dinner (or wedding!), each clutching a tiny posy of flowers or herbs – just paint with a pale colour and write the names on in pen.*

- *These pegs are perfect for hanging up party decorations, so for a really special occasion why not decorate with glitter? Simply paint your pegs with a thick coat of craft glue and sprinkle generously with glitter while it's still wet.*

HOW TO

1. We're only painting one face of each peg, so start by masking off the sides so you don't get paint on them. Stick masking tape all the way around the edges of your peg, aligning the tape with the top edge neatly. Press the masking tape down firmly to make sure paint doesn't sneak underneath.

2. You can either paint a background colour, which will show between your stripes, or leave the bare wood to show through (you can see a mix of both types in the photo). If you're going for a background colour, start by painting the whole face of your peg, allow to dry, then apply a second coat. Once it's completely dry, you're ready to add your stripes. (Acrylic paint dries quickly, so be sure to wash your brush out between each use.)

3. Stick small strips of masking tape at an angle across the face of your peg, creating stripes of different sizes between the tape.

4. Paint in the stripes between your tape – if you're using several colours, paint a few stripes in one colour and then change colour, until all your stripes are painted. Allow to dry then add another coat of paint.

5. Once your second coat is fully dry, remove the tape from the face of your pegs. If you want to add more stripes between the ones you've painted, simply repeat the process masking off different areas.

6. If your pegs are likely to get a lot of use or will be used to hang up washing, apply a coat of clear-drying craft glue to act as a varnish on top of the paint.

7. Once you're happy with your stripes and everything is dry, remove the tape from the sides of your pegs, and voila!

A Cork Peg and Drawstring Bag

I have a row of these in my bathroom full of things like spare soaps and cotton buds, but I also think they'd be great next to a coat rack for gloves and hats! They make a versatile little storage unit for pretty much any space.

MATERIALS AND EQUIPMENT

CORK PEG
M
- 1 cork (Champagne-style corks work best, but regular wine corks are fine, too)
- Acrylic paint
- 1 long nail (it should be at least 1.5 cm [⅝ inch] longer than your cork)

E
- Small paintbrush
- Pencil
- Hammer

DRAWSTRING BAG
M
- Mid- to heavyweight fabric, at least 32 cm x 70 cm (12½ inches x 27½ inches) (I've used a fair trade organic cotton fine corduroy)
- Cotton thread or ribbon to match your fabric
- 150 cm (59 inches) thick string, cord or ribbon (I've used vintage macramé cord for the drawstring)

E
- Tailor's chalk
- Long ruler or tape measure
- Scissors
- Pins
- Sewing machine

MAKE IT YOUR OWN

- *The cork pegs also work well on their own: I have them on the back of almost every door in my flat for hanging up jackets. Or you could create a cluster of them on a wall to hang up your jewellery – part storage, part display!*

- *Similarly, the drawstring bags have endless uses. I've made a giant one, which I use as a laundry sack, a small one to serve as an toiletries bag, and tiny ones for gift bags.*

HOW TO

CORK PEG
1 Start by painting your cork. Don't worry about the top and bottom for now, just give the side two or three coats of paint, letting it dry between each coat.

2 Decide where you would like your bag to hang and mark with a pencil where your cork peg will go. (These pegs work really well on walls and doors, just check first that it's a suitable surface for nailing into. Masonry walls, for instance, may be too hard and some doors may be too thin!)

3 With the cork stood on its flat end on a flat surface, start hammering the long nail through its centre (be careful not to hammer your nail all the way through!). Once your nail is about halfway through, hold your cork up to your pencil mark and continue hammering until only the head of the nail shows and the cork is securely held to the wall.

4 Paint the top of your cork the same colour as the sides to conceal the nail head. Your peg is finished!

DRAWSTRING BAG
1 Using your tailor's chalk, mark out a rectangle 32 cm x 70 cm (12½ inches x 27½ inches) on your fabric. (If you are making lots of bags you may find it quicker to make a template from a piece of card or paper and draw around this.) Cut out your rectangle along the chalk lines.

2 Lay your fabric rectangle face down on a flat surface. Following diagram A, fold narrow triangles 5 cm (2 inches) long at the top and bottom of each of the long sides, pinning them in place. Machine sew, removing the pins as you go (see diagram B).

3 Lay out your rectangle again, still face down. Now fold in 1 cm (⅜ inch) of fabric all the way along one of the short edges, then fold it over by another 2.5 cm (1 inch) and pin in place. Sew just above the bottom edge of the folded-over fabric (see diagram C).

4 Repeat step 3 along the other short edge.

5 Now lay out your rectangle face up, and fold it in half so that the short edges meet at the top. Pin along both sides, up to the folded top (see diagram D). Sew along these edges, 1 cm (⅜ inch) in from the edge, removing the pins as you go and stopping at the folded top.

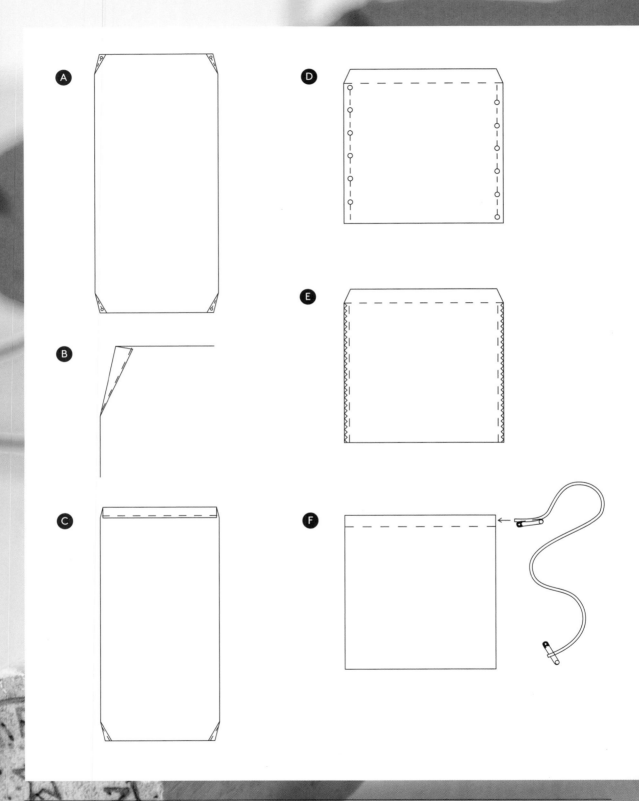

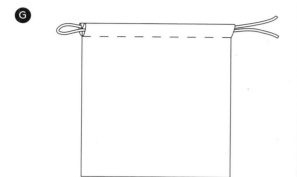

G

6 Set your machine to a zigzag stitch and sew along the outer edge of each side to prevent your seams fraying (see diagram E). Again, be sure not to sew over the folded top edge.

7 Turn your bag inside out.

8 Next we can add the drawstring! Cut your cord or ribbon in half so you end up with two pieces, each 75 cm (29½ inches) long. Take one of the pieces of cord and pin a safety pin across it at one end (this will stop your cord from pulling straight through to the other side as you thread it!). Pin the second safety pin along (not across) the cord at the other end. Use this safety pin to help you thread the cord through one of the folded edges of your bag (see diagram F). Once it is all the way through one side, thread it back through the folded edge on the other side of the bag (see diagram G). Both ends of your cord should now be on the same side of the bag.

9 Repeat with the second piece of cord but in the opposite direction, so that both ends of your second piece of cord end up on the other side of the bag to the first cord (see diagram H).

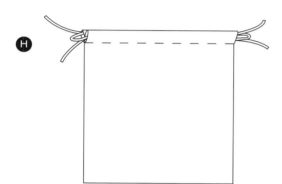

H

10 Once both your cords are in place, remove the safety pins. Holding both ends of one cord together, tie a double knot, then repeat for the other side.

11 Now pull on your knots and your drawstring bag should be working!

12 Once your bag is finished, you can fill it with whatever you need to store (from socks to sunglasses) and hang it on its cork peg!

Painted
Cork
Pinboards

These simple pinboards look great hanging together in a group. I love using them in my studio to keep all my little random bits and pieces of inspiration in some kind of order! By only painting the sides of the boards and a little of the front they add a subtle pop of colour to a space.

MATERIALS AND EQUIPMENT

M
- 1 round cork board 20 cm x 0.6 cm (8 inches x ¼ inch) (or as many as you'd like to make!)
- Acrylic paint

E
- Masking tape
- Cutting mat (or very thick card that your craft knife won't cut through!)
- Craft knife or scalpel
- Small paintbrush
- Hammer and a nail or Velcro tabs for hanging (see step 10)

MAKE IT YOUR OWN

- *These pinboards work really well as a group (either all painted in the same colour or in a mix of colours that complement one another). Try out different ways of hanging them: in a row with the coloured crescents at different angles, tightly clustered together to form one large board, or randomly spaced at different heights ... the options are endless!*

- *Other shapes and sizes of cork boards are available, so you don't have to stick to circles!*

HOW TO

1   The first step is to mask off your cork board so that you can paint the sides without getting any paint on the front. To do this, take small strips of masking tape, (each about 8 cm [3 inches] long) and stick these flat to the front of the cork board all the way around the edge, so they overlap each other and overhang the edge of the board.

2   Once you have masking-taped all the way round the front of your board, turn the board over and place it on a cutting mat. With a craft knife or scalpel cut the overhanging tape away all the way around the edge of the board (be careful not to cut the cork!).

3   Turn your board back over and gently press down the masking tape to make sure it is sealed along the edges. Doing this will ensure the paint won't be able to find its way underneath and onto the front of the board.

4   Using a small paintbrush, paint the side of your board (don't worry about getting paint on the back of the board – this won't show when you hang it up). To prevent any paint sticking to your work surface, sit your board face down on top of an upturned cup or jar while it dries.

5   Allow the first coat of paint to dry then apply a second coat.

6   Once your second coat of paint is dry, carefully remove the masking tape, leaving the front of your board paint free! Now you're ready to paint the crescent of colour on the front.

7   Stick a strip of masking tape across the front of your cork board, marking out the small crescent segment you'll paint. Gently press the masking tape down to make sure you get a crisp edge.

8   Paint the crescent the same colour as the side. Allow to dry then add a second coat of paint.

9   Once the paint is completely dry remove the masking-tape strip.

10 Your pinboard is now ready to hang! Depending on your walls, you could use a small nail hammered through the top of the pinboard (about 1 cm [⅜ inch] from the top edge) and directly into the wall behind, or else Velcro sticky tabs are a great alternative if you want to avoid using nails.

Cork Pinboard with a Flower Garland

This little decorated pinboard is a great way to add a bold floral touch to any space. You could use it for pinning all sorts of things, from receipts in your home office to notes and reminders in your kitchen!

MATERIALS AND EQUIPMENT

M
- 1 round cork board, 20 x 1 cm (8 x ⅜ inch) or two thinner boards glued together (the board needs to be thick enough so that you can push your pins all the way in to hold the flowers in place)
- A4 sheets of thin card in your choice of colours
- Map pins (I chose white ones)

E
- Pencil
- Scissors
- Craft knife or scalpel
- Cutting mat (or very thick card that your craft knife won't cut through!)
- Hammer and a nail or Velcro tabs for hanging (see step 6)

MAKE IT YOUR OWN

- You could try folding small origami flowers instead of cutting them from card (you can find a wealth of origami instructions online).

- Pinboards aren't just for notes – how about using them in your bedroom to organize your jewellery (large pushpins are perfect for hanging jewellery from) or to display your photos!

HOW TO

1   First, design your flowers and leaves. You can trace or copy the templates on page 40, or make up your own. Make sure some of your flowers have petals that can be folded in a little, to add a bit of depth (I've done this with the long petals of the large round flowers).

2   In pencil, draw your flowers and leaves on your chosen colours of card (I've used a different colour for each type of flower and leaf). Cut out the basic shapes with scissors, then use a craft knife or scalpel and a cutting mat to cut out the smaller details.

3   Turn your flowers and leaves over so that any pencil lines still showing are on the back.

4   Play around with placing your flowers and leaves along one side of the front of your board (I find they look best if I start in the middle and work out towards the top and bottom, overlapping the leaves and adding the flowers on top).

5   Once you are happy with your floral cluster, pin each leaf in place at its base, and each flower at its centre.

6   Your pinboard is now ready to hang! Depending on your walls, you could use a small nail hammered through the top of the pinboard (about 1 cm [⅜ inch] from the top edge) and directly into the wall behind, or else Velcro sticky tabs are a great alternative if you want to avoid using nails.

7   If you get bored of your pinboard or want to change your colour scheme you can simply unpin your flowers and make new ones!

Template

Cube
Bookends

*A geode may not be the first thing
that springs to mind when you see
these cube bookends but, honestly,
that's where my design process
started! I love the way geodes
have a seemingly glowing, coloured
interior encased in solid, neutral rock,
and I wanted to make something to
achieve the same effect.*
*I've lost count of the number of
colour combinations I tried until
I found the right one: mushroom
grey with the brightest pink.*

MATERIALS AND EQUIPMENT

There are lots of places you can get wood or MDF cut to size – just search online for somewhere close to you.

M
- 4 blocks of 1.8 cm (¾ inch) thick wood or MDF cut to 10 cm x 10 cm (4 inches x 4 inches)
- 4 blocks of 1.8 cm (¾ inch) thick wood or MDF cut to 6.4 cm x 10 cm (2½ inches x 4 inches)
- Eco-friendly acrylic paint in pale grey and bright pink, or your choice of colours
- Eco-friendly wood glue

E
- Old newspapers to protect your work surface
- Sandpaper
- Medium paintbrush
- Masking tape
- Small paintbrush

HOW TO

1   Set out one of your 10 cm x 10 cm (4 inches x 4 inches) wooden blocks flat on a piece of newspaper.

2   Now take one of your 6.4 cm x 10 cm (2½ inch x 4 inch) blocks and apply wood glue along one of the long edges. Place the glue edge on one side of your square block (see diagram A) and line it up exactly with the edges.

3   Do the same with another 6.4 cm x 10 cm (2½ inch x 4 inch) block on the opposite side of the square block (see diagram B).

4   Next, apply glue to the top edges of your two glued-down blocks (being careful not to move them) and place a second 10 cm x 10 cm (4 inch x 4 inch) block on top (see diagram C). Press the top block down firmly (don't worry if some glue spills out!).

5   Check that all your edges line up neatly and make any adjustments while the glue is still wet. Clean off any excess glue gently with a tissue (on the inside and outside).

6   Repeat this with your remaining four blocks for your second bookend and leave both cubes to dry (ideally overnight).

7   Once the glue is completely dry, sand any rough edges or slight overlaps.

8   With your grey acrylic, paint the sides and edges of your cubes. You can do this in stages, letting parts dry and then turning the cubes over (so they are never sat on a wet side!). Build up coats of paint in this way, until you have a smooth, opaque finish. Leave to dry completely.

9   To paint the inside of the cube, first mask the outside edges on either side with masking tape. Using your second colour, paint the inside of each cube, again, building up several coats to create a strong, solid colour.

10 Once the inside colour is dry, carefully remove the masking tape. To get a really neat edge between the two colours you may have to use a fine brush to go over any specks of paint that have found their way under the masking tape.

11 Once all the paint is dry, your bookends are ready to use.

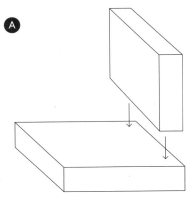

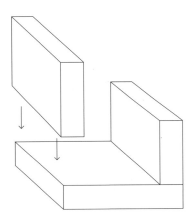

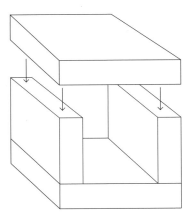

MAKE IT YOUR OWN

- You can pick up gorgeous, vintage wooden bookends (on eBay or in secondhand or charity shops) which look great as they are, or you can spruce them up with a couple of coats of bright acrylic paint (like the red pair in the photo opposite).

- Once you've made the cubes, they are something of a blank canvas that you could decorate in any number of ways. You could mask and paint them with stripes (like the Striped Clothes Pegs project on page 26), or coat the inside with glue and cover it in glitter – the possibilities are endless.

NESTING

This part of the book is all about comfort. It's about your home being a place of safety and warmth. I could write a whole book on cushions alone, so it was tough to choose just a couple of designs to feature here. In the end, I decided on two that seemed to best represent the main aspects of my taste: bright, folky and clashing, and simple, clean and geometric. The Wool Embroidered Cushion on page 54 falls into the first category, and I think it would add a perfect touch of texture and pattern to an otherwise quite minimal setting. Cushions or blankets are often at their best used in this way – as a little rogue element!

Corner Contrast Cushion

I always think of cushions as the perfect quick-fix way to make a space feel like home (even if it's a rented studio flat that you're not allowed to decorate!). They're quick to make, easy to change around and provide instant comfort.

MATERIALS AND EQUIPMENT

Makes one cushion.

M

- Mid-weight cotton fabric in two contrasting colours:
- Front fabric at least 45 cm x 45 cm (18¾ inches x 18¾ inches)
- Backing/corner fabric at least 100 cm x 90 cm (39½ inches x 35½ inches)
- Cotton thread to match either of your fabrics
- 40 cm (15¾ inch) square cushion pad

E

- 1 sheet of card or paper at least 40 cm x 40 cm (15¾ inches x 15¾ inches)
- Long ruler or tape measure
- Pencil
- Scissors
- Tailor's chalk
- Pins
- Sewing machine
- Iron

HOW TO

1   Measure and cut out a piece of card or paper to make a square 40 cm x 40 cm (15¾ inches x 15¾ inches). From the bottom left corner of this square mark a point 18 cm (7⅛ inches) up the left side. Mark a second point 27cm (10⅝ inches) from the bottom left corner along the bottom of the square. Now draw a line between these two points with your ruler to form a triangle and cut along the line. These two pieces are the templates for the front of your cushion (see diagram A).

2   Lay out the fabric for the main part of the front of your cushion on a flat surface with the right side facing down. Using tailor's chalk, draw around the template (this is the square with its corner cut off). Cut around your shape 1.5 cm (⅝ inch) outside of the chalk lines.

3   Next, cut out two 43 cm x 63 cm (17 inch x 25 inch) rectangles from your backing fabric. *(If you are making lots of cushions you may find it quicker to make a template from a piece of card or paper and draw around this.)* On the remaining piece of backing fabric draw around the corner-piece template (the triangle) and cut it out 1.5 cm (⅝ inch) outside the chalk lines.

4   Now that we have all the pieces cut for the cushion we just need to sew them together! Start by laying out the main front piece of the cushion with its corresponding corner piece, right sides facing up. As though folding along an imaginary seam where the two pieces of fabric meet, lay the corner piece right side facing down on top of the rest of the square, so that their diagonal edges meet (see diagrams B and C). Pin along the diagonal, 1.5 cm (⅝ inch) from the edge, then unfold and turn over to check that the corner piece is lined up correctly to match up with the rest of the chalk outline (see diagram D).

5   Machine stitch along the pinned edge, 1.5 cm (⅝ inch) from the edge, removing the pins as you go. Once sewn, unfold the corner and press with an iron. Your square is complete!

6   Next, take one of the pieces of fabric that you cut for the back of your cushion. Lay it on a flat surface, with the right side facing down, and fold it in half so that the shorter edges meet. Give the folded edge a press with your iron. Repeat with the second piece.

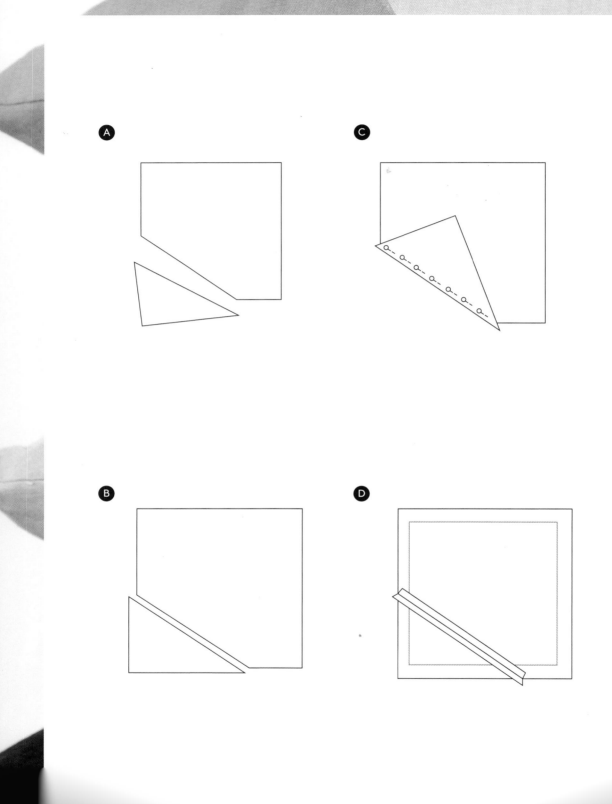

7   Place one of the backing pieces in front of you with its folded edge to the left. Hold the second piece with its folded edge to the right and place it on top of the first piece so that the folded edges overlap in the middle by 20 cm (8 inches). This will form a square 43 cm x 43 cm (17 inches x 17 inches).

8   Lay the front panel of your cushion face down on top of this square, so that all the edges line up neatly. Pin all the way round the edge of the fabric, 1.5 cm (⅝ inch) from the edge.

9   Sew around the fabric, 1.5 cm (⅝ inch) from the edge, removing the pins as you go.

10 To make sure your cushions have nice pointy corners, cut across each of the corners of your seam, a little way from the corners of your stitching (see the diagram on page 9). Trim and neaten the rest of your seam to about 1 cm (⅜ inch) all the way round.

11 Now turn your cushion cover inside out and fill it with the cushion pad.

MAKE IT YOUR OWN

- If you fancy a hint of pattern you could use a patterned fabric just for the corner section and a plain fabric (picking out one of the colours from the pattern) for the rest of the cushion.

- Vary the look by using different templates for the corner sections, ranging from a tiny corner to half the square! Or how about a strip of colour instead of a corner?

Wool-embroidered Cushion

Embroidery is a fairly time consuming pursuit, but it is the perfect craft accompaniment to watching television (I made these while watching David Attenborough nature documentaries – I think maybe it shows!).

MATERIALS AND EQUIPMENT

Makes one cushion.

M

- Mid-weight cotton fabric, at least 110 x 90 cm
  (43½ x 35½ inches)
- Wool in various colours (I've used use Debbie
  Bliss Eco Baby and Eco Aran made from fair
  trade organic cotton)
- Cotton thread to match your fabric
- 40 cm (15¾ inch) square cushion pad

E

- Tailor's chalk
- Long ruler or tape measure
- Scissors
- 30 cm (12 inch) diameter embroidery ring
- Large embroidery needle
- Iron
- Pins
- Sewing machine

HOW TO

1   Measure and cut out a 43 cm x 43 cm (17 inch x 17 inch) square
    from your fabric. (If you are making lots of cushions you may find it
    quicker to make templates from a piece of card or paper and draw
    around these.)

2   Next cut out two 43 cm x 63 cm (17 inch x 25 inch) rectangles
    from your fabric.

3   The 43 cm x 43 cm (17 inch x 17 inch) square will be the front of
    your cushion so lay this on a flat surface with the right side facing
    up, ready to draw out your embroidery pattern. You can copy one
    of the patterns from pages 58–63 or make up your own. Draw
    your pattern in tailor's chalk (you don't have to be too precise, this
    is just to help guide you as you sew). Make sure your embroidery
    stops at least 3 cm (1¼ inches) from the edges, to allow for
    the seam.

4   Next, stretch your fabric over your embroidery ring with the pattern
    within the ring area. (If your embroidered area is larger than the
    ring area you'll need to do this in sections, moving the ring to
    different areas of your fabric as you go.) Place the smaller inner
    ring on a hard surface, lay your fabric over this and push the larger
    ring over the top, stretching the fabric over the smaller ring. Then
    tighten the screw on the larger ring to hold it in place.

5   Now you're ready to begin your embroidery. Choose the first wool
    colour you would like to work with. Cut a length of wool (roughly
    the length of your arm) and thread your needle, tying a knot in
    the end of the wool. The leaf and starflower designs on pages
    58–59 are sewn with a simple running or backstitch (using a single
    stitch for each facet of the zigzag outline). The fan shape on page
    60–63and the large firework flowers on pages 58–59 are sewn in
    star or eyelet stitch (each line of the fan or flower is a single stitch,
    sewn from the outside edge to the centre).

6   Once your embroidery is complete, remove the ring and give your
    fabric a quick iron. Now you can sew the cushion together!

7   Take one of the pieces of fabric that you cut for the back of your
    cushion. Lay it on a flat surface with the right side facing down and
    fold it in half so that the shorter edges meet. Give the folded edge
    a press with your iron. Repeat with the second piece.

8   Place one of the backing pieces in front of you with its folded edge to the left. Hold the second piece with its folded edge to the right and place it on top of the first piece so that the folded edges overlap in the middle by 20 cm (8 inches). This will form a square 43 cm x 43 cm (17 inches x 17 inches).

9   Lay the front panel of your cushion face down on top of this square, so that all the edges line up neatly. Pin all the way round the edge of the fabric, 1.5 cm (⅝ inch) from the edge.

10 Sew around the fabric, 1.5 cm (⅝ inch) from the edge, removing the pins as you go.

11 To make sure your cushions have nice pointy corners, cut across each of the corners of your seam, a little way from the corners of your stitching (see the diagram on page 9). Trim and neaten the rest of your seam to about 1 cm (⅜ inch) all the way round.

12 Now turn your cushion cover inside out and fill it with the cushion pad.

MAKE IT YOUR OWN

- *There's no limit to what kind of patterns you can embroider, so why not make up your own? The motifs I designed were inspired by folk-style vintage embroidery, but any line drawing, pattern or text could form the basis for your embroidery.*

- *I've just used simple straight stitches here, but there are loads of beautiful stitches out there you can use to add interest and texture to your embroidery (you can find fantastic guides online).*

Template

Template – left

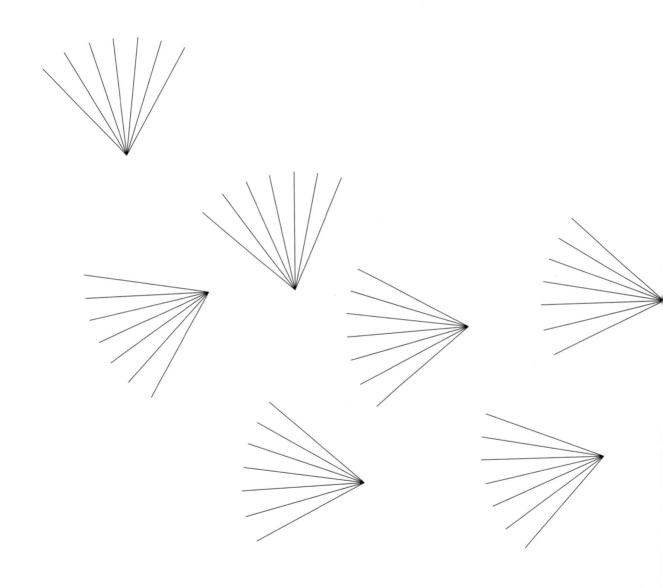

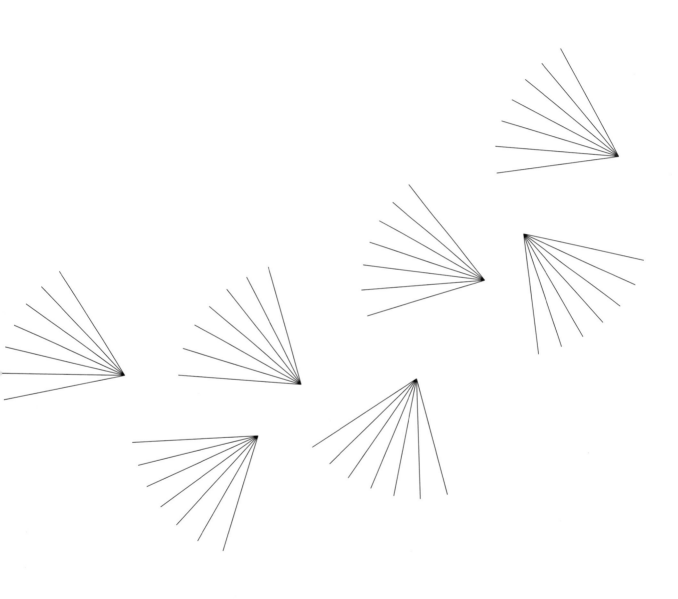

Template – right

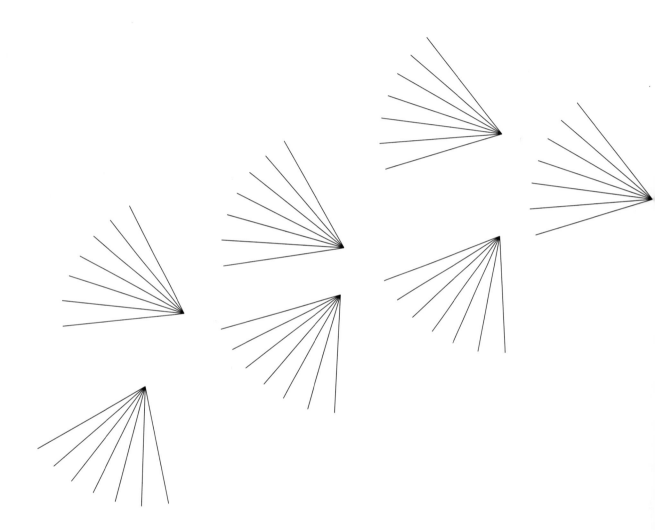

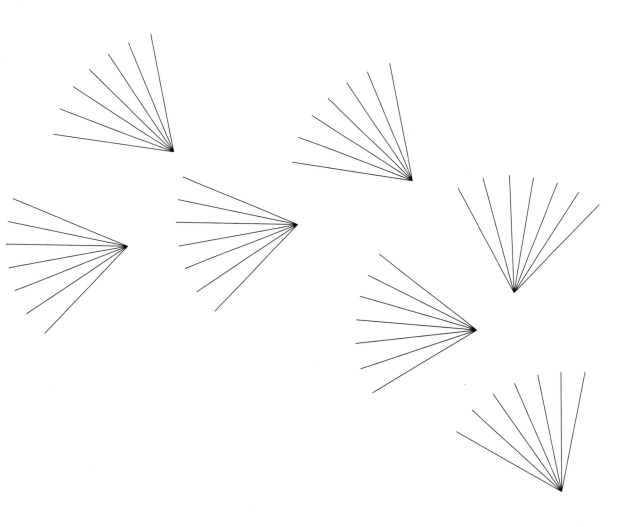

Modern Quilted Blanket

I wanted to create a simplified, modern take on the geometric patterns of traditional patchwork quilts. This was partly for a bold, striking aesthetic and partly to design something that can be made in an afternoon rather than over many months!

Your blanket will end up measuring around 87 cm x 115 cm (34 inches x 45 inches), the perfect size for evenings spent curled up reading or in front of the television – I leave one permanently draped over my sofa ready to grab.

MATERIALS AND EQUIPMENT

The key to this design is your choice of colours. I've used a deep burgundy and navy blue for the main colours, as these are very similar in tone. This gives the vivid bright pink of the stray brightly coloured triangle (and the back of the blanket) all the more impact. See page 71 for how your finished blanket should look.

M

- Navy blue mid-weight cotton fabric, at least 70 cm x 110 cm (27½ inches x 43½ inches)
- Burgundy mid-weight cotton fabric, at least 70 cm x 110 cm (27½ inches x 43½ inches)
- Bright pink mid-weight cotton fabric, at least 150cm x 120 cm (59 inches x 47¼ inches)
- Cotton batting, at least 90 cm x 120 cm (35½ inches x 47¼ inches)
- Cotton thread in navy

E

- 1 sheet of card, at least 33.5 cm x 33.5 cm (13¼ inches x 13¼ inches)
- Long ruler
- Pencil
- Scissors
- Tailor's chalk
- Pins
- Sewing machine
- Iron

HOW TO

1   First make a template to draw out your squares (which will later become your triangles!). Cut out a card square 33.5 cm x 33.5 cm (13¼ inches x 13¼ inches).

2   Lay out your navy blue fabric on a table or hard surface, with the right side facing down. Draw around your card template with tailor's chalk to mark out six squares.

3   Repeat for the burgundy fabric.

4   You also need to mark out one square on your pink fabric (make sure you do this close to a corner so that you leave enough pink fabric for backing the blanket).

5   Cut out your fabric squares neatly along your chalk lines.

6   Using a long ruler, draw a line with your tailor's chalk diagonally across each fabric square, from corner to corner, dividing each square into two triangles.

7   Cut each square in half to form 12 navy blue triangles, 12 burgundy triangles and 2 pink triangles.

8   Remove one burgundy triangle and one pink triangle (these are spare, so save them for a future project or a second blanket!).

9   Lay out your first navy blue triangle with its right side facing up, and place your pink triangle face down on top of it, so all the edges match up.

10 Pin along the longest edge, 1 cm (⅜ inch) in from the edge of the fabric (see diagram A).

11 Now do the same with the remaining triangles, matching up each navy blue triangle with a burgundy triangle.

12 Thread your sewing machine with navy cotton and sew each pair of triangles along their longest edge, 1 cm (⅜ inch) from the edge of the fabric, removing the pins as you go.

13 Once you've sewn together each pair of triangles, fold each one out to form a square. Press with an iron along the seam to flatten it out and trim off the points of the seam that stick out from behind (see diagram B). So now you've gone from squares to triangles and back to squares again.

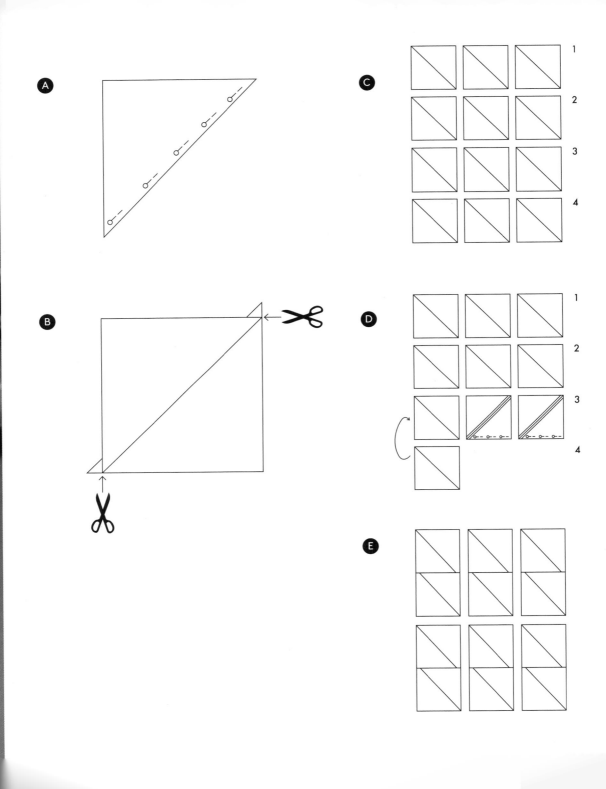

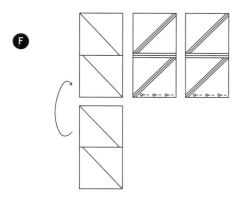

F

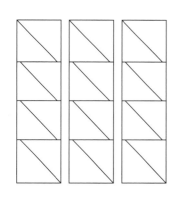

G

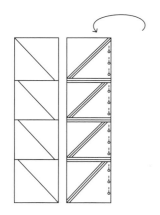

H

14　Next we need to sew the squares together. To make sure you get the pattern of different coloured triangles in the right order I find it best to start by laying out your squares in the final formation (see diagram C).

15　Now, as though folding along an imaginary seam between the squares, lay a square from row 4 face down on the square above. Pin the two squares together along the bottom edge of the fabric. Repeat this for the other squares in row 4 (see diagram D).

16　Repeat step 15 with the squares in row 2, placing them face down on top of the squares in row 1 and pinning along the bottom edge.

17　Sew each pair of squares along their pinned edge, 1 cm (⅜ inch) from the edge of the fabric, removing the pins as you go.

18　Once you've sewn together each pair of squares, fold them out again along their seam and press with an iron to flatten them out.

19　Lay your rectangles out again in the final formation. You should now have two rows with three rectangles in each (see diagram E).

20　As you did with the squares, take each rectangle from the bottom row and place it face down on the rectangle above (as though folding along an imaginary seam between the rectangles), lining up all the edges (see diagram F). Pin along the bottom short edge of the fabric.

21　Sew each pair of rectangles along their pinned short edge, 1 cm (⅜ inch) from the edge of the fabric, removing the pins as you go.

22　You should now have three long strips, ready to sew together! In the same way as before, lay these out in the final formation (see diagram G).

23　Place the right-hand strip face down on top of the middle strip, lining up all the edges (see diagram H) and pin along the right-hand long edge.

I

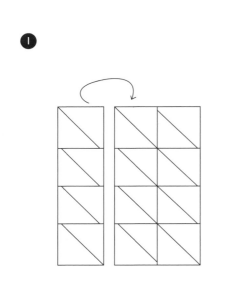

K

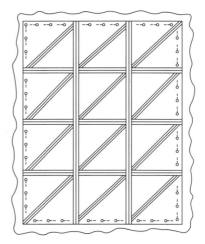

J

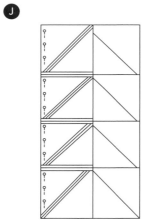

L

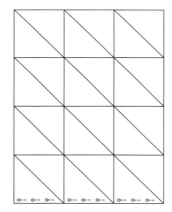

24 Sew the two strips together along the pinned edge, 1 cm (⅜ inch) from the edge of the fabric, removing the pins as you go.

25 Unfold and press with an iron. Lay out your pieces again.

26 Now place the left-hand strip face down over the central strip (see diagram I), lining up the left-hand long edge and pinning all the way along the long edge of the fabric (see diagram J).

27 Sew as before, removing the pins as you go.

28 Unfold and press with an iron. The front panel of your blanket is complete!

29 Now, you need to make a sandwich of fabrics and batting! Lay out your batting on a flat surface (I usually do this on the floor, as my table isn't big enough!). Lay your pink backing fabric on top of this with the right side facing up, and lay your finished front panel face down on top of this (I know this might seem like the wrong order, but trust me, it'll work out right!).

30 Making sure the three layers line up, pin the layers together all the way around your front panel (see diagram K).

31 Now that your layers are held together, trim away any excess backing and batting material.

32 Starting on one of the longer sides, sew along three of the sides 1 cm (⅜ inch) from the edge of the front panel, removing the pins as you go. Make sure you leave the fourth side unsewn.

33 To give your blanket neater corners, cut across each one, a little way from the corners of your stitching (see the diagram on page 9).

34 Now turn your fabric sandwich inside out making sure you end up with the fabrics on the outside and the batting on the inside! Gently poke out the corners from the inside with a pencil (be careful not to poke too hard!). Give your blanket a press with a warm iron.

35 Along the open side, fold in 1 cm (⅜ inch) of the backing fabric and batting all the way along the bottom edge. Then fold in 1 cm (⅜ inch) of the front panel along the top edge. Pin in place 0.5 cm (¼ inch) from the edge so that the two edges are neatly lined up (see diagram L).

36 Always keeping 0.5 cm (¼ inch) in from the edge, sew along the pinned edge following the pins and removing them as you go. Continue stitching along the other 3 sides of the blanket. When you reach the folded edge again overlap the stitching by 1 cm (⅜ inch) or so to secure the ends, and you're done!

MAKE IT YOUR OWN

- *This would make a wonderful house-warming gift in a friend's favourite colours, or a new-baby gift in pastel shades.*

- *For a more traditional patchwork look you could use an assortment of patterned vintage fabrics – a great way to use up small remnants!*

- *If you're short on time, a quicker version can be made using a 30 cm x 30 cm (12 inch x 12 inch) card template, and by leaving the squares whole (just cut out one less burgundy square and miss out steps 6 to 13).*

Pompom Blanket

If you want to have a go at a
blanket project, but don't feel ready
to tackle all those triangles in the
Modern Quilted Blanket project
on page 64, this one's super simple,
but the pompoms make it look
really special.

Your finished blanket will be around
97 cm x 115 cm (38½ inches x
45 inches), plus pompoms!

MATERIALS AND EQUIPMENT

As this blanket is a fairly plain design, I wanted to use a fabric with a bit of texture to it to add some extra interest, so I chose an organic cotton twill in contrasting colours for the front and back. See page 70 for how your finished blanket should look.

M

- Wool in red, bright blue and plum (I've used Debbie Bliss Fair Trade Organic Cotton)
- Cotton batting, at least 100 cm x 120 cm (39½ inches x 47¼ inches)
- Navy blue cotton twill fabric, at least 100 cm x 120 cm (39½ inches x 47¼ inches)
- Off-white cotton twill fabric, at least 100 cm x 120 cm (39½ inches x 47¼ inches)
- Cotton thread in navy

E

- 2.5 cm (1 inch) pompom maker*
- Sharp scissors
- Tape measure
- Tailor's chalk
- Pins
- Sewing machine
- Iron
- Large embroidery needle

*I use Clover Pom-Pom Makers as they're quick and give consistent, neat results, especially for making small pompoms, but if you'd prefer to do it the old-school way with two pieces of card, that's absolutely fine too (you can find loads of instructions online). Clover Pom-Pom Makers are available from online craft stores.

HOW TO

1   We'll start with the most fun part: making the pompoms! You'll need 7 pompoms in total: 3 red, 2 blue and 2 plum. Take your pompom maker and fold out one set of the 'arms' – holding the pompom maker in one hand begin winding your first wool colour around the arch in the centre of the arms. Continue winding, moving gradually from one end of the arch to the other and back again, until the arch is full.

2   Once full, close the arms and snip the end of your wool thread.

3   Fold out the opposite set of arms and repeat steps 1 and 2.

4   Now cut a length of wool 20 cm (8 inches) long and set to one side.

5   Take your sharp scissors and snip along the middle of the wool all the way around your pompom maker – be sure to cut every single strand of wool.

6   Now take your 20 cm (8 inch) length of wool and tie this around your pompom maker, following the gap you have just cut. Pull firmly and tie in a tight double knot.

7   Unfold both sets of arms and pull the two sides of your pompom maker apart. Voila, you have a pompom!

8   Roll your pompom gently between your hands to fluff it up and use your scissors to trim any long bits of wool (be careful not to cut the long thread you tied around the middle though, as you'll need that later!).

9   Repeat steps 1 to 8 until you have 7 pompoms. Now you can start the blanket.

10 Firstly, lay out your batting on a flat surface (I usually do this on the floor so I have plenty of space). Place your navy fabric face up on top of your batting, and place your off-white fabric face down on top of this (I know this might seem like the wrong order, but trust me, it'll work out right!).

11 Making sure the three layers of your fabric sandwich line up, pin the layers together all the way around the edge (see diagram A).

12 Now that your layers are held together, trim away any excess backing and batting material.

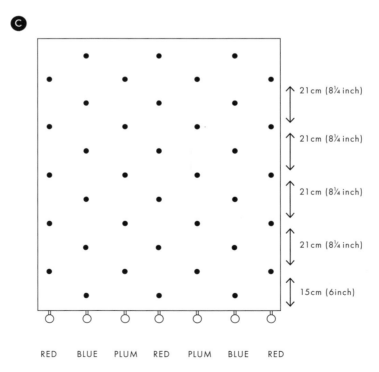

21cm (8¼ inch)

21cm (8¼ inch)

21cm (8¼ inch)

21cm (8¼ inch)

15cm (6inch)

RED   BLUE   PLUM   RED   PLUM   BLUE   RED

13 Starting on one of the longer sides, sew along three sides 1 cm (⅜ inch) from the edges of the front panel, removing the pins as you go. Make sure you leave the fourth side unsewn!

14 To give your blanket neater corners, cut across each one, a little way from the corners of your stitching (see the diagram on page 9).

15 Now turn your fabric sandwich inside out, making sure you end up with the fabrics on the outside and the batting on the inside! Gently poke out the corners from the inside with a pencil (be careful not to poke too hard!). Give your blanket a press with a warm iron.

16 Along the open side, fold in 2 cm (¾ inch) of off-white fabric and batting all the way along the bottom edge. Then fold in 2 cm (¾ inch) of the navy blue fabric along the top edge. Pin in place 1 cm (⅜ inch) from the edge so that the top and bottom edges are neatly lined up (see diagram B).

17 Along your pinned edge, measure 4 cm (1½ inches) in from the right-hand side. At this point, poke the long threads of one of your red pompoms into the open edge, until roughly 2 cm (¾ inch) remains on the outside with the pompom hanging down. Pin in place.

18 Repeat this on the left-hand side with the next red pompom and then in the middle with the last red pompom.

19 Now add your blue and plum pompoms in the same way, spacing them evenly in the gaps between the red pompoms, so they end up in this order: red, blue, plum, red, plum, blue, red.

20 Once all your pompoms are pinned in place, sew along your pinned edge, 1 cm (⅝ inch) from the edge, removing the pins as you go. This will fix the pompoms in place.

21 Now all that's left to do is to add the little wool knots that give the blanket its lovely quilted look. Begin by measuring and marking where each knot will go on the navy blue side of your blanket (see diagram C). The colour of each column of knots matches the pompom at the bottom of the blanket.

22 Take a length of your red wool (about 40 cm [16 inches]) and thread your large needle. At the mark for your first red knot, push your needle through from the front to the back and make a stitch about 1 cm (⅝ inch) long. Tie the two ends of your

stitch together and make a double knot. Cut away the excess wool, leaving 1 cm (⅜ inch) tufts on the knot.

23 Repeat this with red wool for all the knots in that column, then for the other two red columns.

24 Do the same with the blue and plum columns until all your knots are tied.

MAKE IT YOUR OWN

- *There's no such thing as too many pompoms! Rather than a somewhat reserved 7 pompoms, you could fill the whole edge with as many as you like. You could vary the sizes and colours too.*

- *If pompoms aren't quite what you're after, how about tassels instead? (You can find instructions for making tassels on page 104.)*

- *Or, if pompoms are most certainly what you're after, you could incorporate them into other projects, like cushion covers or garlands ...*

Blanket Basket

This fabric basket is designed to store your lovely blankets when they're not being used, but it works just as well as a knitting basket or for books or slippers ...

MATERIALS AND EQUIPMENT

To give your basket a bit of structure it's important to use fairly heavy fabrics. I've chosen a herringbone fabric for the outside (because I love the pattern and texture) and a thicker texweave cotton for the inside to create contrast and for extra body.

M

- Patterned heavyweight cotton fabric for the outside, at least 55 cm x 75 cm (21¾ inches x 29½ inches)
- Cotton thread to match your outer fabric
- Plain heavyweight cotton fabric for the inside, at least 45 cm x 65 cm (17¾ inches x 25½ inches)

E

- Tape measure
- Tailor's chalk
- Scissors
- Pins
- Sewing machine
- Iron

HOW TO

1 Spread out your outer fabric on a flat surface and measure and cut a strip 10 cm x 50 cm (4 inches x 20 inches) and a rectangle 43 cm x 74 cm (17 inches x 29 ⅛ inches). Put the long strip to one side.

2 With the fabric rectangle right side facing up, fold it in half, so that the shorter edges meet at the top and pin together along the two sides (see diagram A).

3 Sew along the two sides, 1 cm (⅜ inch) from the edge, removing the pins as you go.

4 Now we need to square off the bottom corners to create the cube shape. Hold the fabric 'envelope' you've sewn in front of you with the open edge facing up and one of the side seams pointing away from you. Pull the two sides of the envelope away from each other. Allow the seam that's facing away from you to flatten down towards you (see diagram B). You want to end up with a triangle pointing away from you and the seam running central.

5 From the tip of the triangle, measure 7 cm (2¾ inches) along your seam and mark this point with tailor's chalk. Then, using this mark as a guide, draw a line all the way across, at a right angle to the seam (I judge the right angle by eye, but you could use a set square if you'd like to be exact). Pin along this line (see diagram C).

6 Turn your fabric round and repeat this on the other corner, then sew along your pinned lines, removing the pins as you go. Cut your triangle corners off, 1 cm (⅜ inch) from the lines you've just sewn (see diagram D).

7 Turn this outer basket inside out (so that the seams are on the inside).

8 Now take your inner fabric and measure and cut a rectangle 43 cm x 62 cm (17 inches x 24½ inches).

9 Repeat steps 2 to 6 for your inner fabric – don't turn it inside out.

10 Stand up your outer fabric basket and tuck your inner basket inside so that all the corners meet and they fit neatly together (the outer layer will come up about 5 cm [2 inches] higher than the inner one).

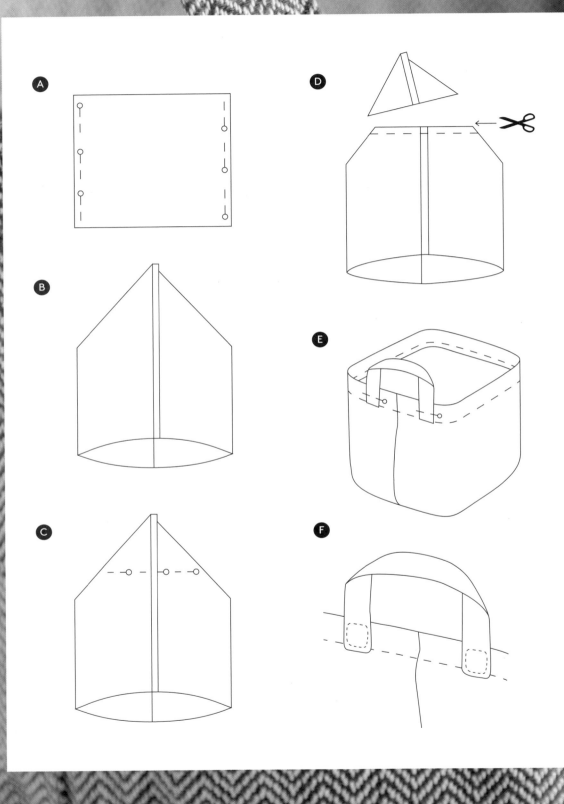

11   Next, fold the rim of the outer layer over by about 2.5 cm (1 inch), then over again (now over the rim of the inner layer) by another 2.5 cm (1 inch). Pin in place. Sew all the way round the basket, 0.5 cm (¼ inch) from the bottom of the folded edge (which will be about 2 cm [¾ inch] from the top edge), removing the pins as you go.

12   Now we just need to add the handles! Start by taking the long strip you cut at the beginning and cutting this in half to form two shorter strips, each 10 cm by 25 cm (4 inches x 10 inches).

13   Lay one of your strips face down on a flat surface. Fold the ends over by roughly 1 cm (⅜ inch). Press the folds with an iron, so they stay in place.

14   Next, fold over the long sides of your strip, so they meet along the middle. Press in place with an iron (and make sure your ends are still folded in).

15   Now fold along the length of the strip, so that the two long edges meet. Press with an iron and pin in place. Your folded strip should now be roughly 2.5 cm (1 inch) wide by 23 cm (9 inches) long.

16   Sew all the way around the edges of your folded strip of fabric, 0.4 cm (⅛ inch) from the edge, removing the pins as you go.

17   Repeat steps 13 to 16 with your other strip and your handles will be ready.

18   Take one of your handles and pin the ends in place on the outside of your basket so each end is 4 cm (1½ inches) away from the side seam and 3 cm (1¼ inch) below the rim of the basket (see diagram E). Repeat this on the opposite side with the second handle.

19   To sew the handles in place, sew along the end of a handle (0.4 cm [⅛ inch] from the edge), then up the handle for 2 cm (¾ inch), across the handle, then down by 2 cm (¾ inch) and across the bottom edge again to form a 2 cm (¾ inch) sewn square (see diagram F). Repeat this on each end of both handles. (You may have to sew this bit by hand if your sewing machine isn't powerful enough to sew through all those layers of heavy fabric.)

MAKE IT YOUR OWN

- *This project can easily be scaled up to make a laundry basket or toy storage, just make sure you use fabrics that are heavy enough to hold their shape – upholstery fabrics are ideal.*

- *If you have storage space under a shelf or piece of furniture, you could make a set of baskets to fit the space exactly – that's one of the joys of making things yourself!*

Ribbon
Quilted
Seat Pad

For me, homeware is at its best when it is both practical and decorative at the same time, and this seat pad seems to fit the bill! I feel there's something of the 1920s in its elegant geometric pattern and the contrast of textures(I was reading an F Scott Fitzgerald novel at the time that I designed this, which may have something to do with it!).

If you're making a set you could choose one colour combination, or a different one for each pad. I chose a clashing combination of bright pink and deep red, which always makes me feel happy.

MATERIALS AND EQUIPMENT

*This makes one standard 40 cm x 40 cm
(15¾ inches x 15¾ inches) seat pad, which will
fit most chairs, but you can adjust the measurements
if you have especially large or small seats!*

M

- Heavyweight cotton fabric, at least 45 cm x
  90 cm (17¾ inches x 35½ inches) (I've used
  an organic cotton twill that's hard-wearing
  without being rough)
- Cotton batting, at least 45 cm x 45 cm (18 inches
  x 18 inches), or 45 cm x 90 cm (18 inches x
  35½ inches) if you want to double it up (see
  step 3)
- Cotton thread to match your fabric
- 5 m (5½ yards) of 2.5 cm (1 inch) wide ribbon
  (I've used vintage ribbon here, as I prefer the
  texture to a lot of new ribbons – and it's always
  good to use up old materials.)

E

- Card or paper at least 40 cm x 40 cm
  (15¾ inches x 15¾ inches)
- Pencil
- Long ruler or tape measure
- Scissors
- Tailor's chalk
- Pins
- Sewing machine
- Iron

HOW TO

1   To make your template, measure and cut out a card or paper
    square 40 cm x 40 cm (15¾ inches x 15¾ inches).

2   Lay out your fabric on a flat surface, face down, and use your
    template and tailor's chalk to mark out two squares 40 cm x 40 cm
    (15¾ inch x 15¾ inch), leaving at least 3 cm (1¼ inch) between
    each one. Cut around your two squares 1.5 cm (⅝ inch) outside
    the chalk lines (to allow for your seam).

3   Lay out your batting. (If your batting is quite thin you may want to
    double it up for a softer seat pad!)

4   Place one of your fabric squares face up on top of your batting and
    place the second fabric square on top, face down, so all the edges
    line up neatly.

5   Pin all the way around the edge of the fabric squares, following
    your chalk outline, making sure to pin through both layers of fabric
    and the batting.

6   Trim your batting to the same size as your fabric.

7   Thread your sewing machine with the same colour thread as your
    fabric. Sew along three sides 1.5 cm (⅝ inch) in from the edges,
    removing the pins as you go. Make sure you leave the fourth side
    unsewn!

8   To give your seat pad neater corners, cut across each one,
    a little way from the corners of your stitching (see the diagram
    on page 9).

9   Turn your fabric envelope inside out, making sure to end up with
    the batting on the inside! (Sometimes the corners need a little help,
    so you might want to poke them out gently with a pencil.) Give
    your seat pad a press with a warm iron to flatten it out a little.

10 Along the open side, fold in 2 cm (¾ inch) of fabric and batting
    all the way along the bottom edge. Then fold in 2 cm (¾ inch) of
    the fabric along the top edge. Pin in place so that the two edges
    are neatly lined up, leaving about 4 cm (1½ inches) unpinned at
    each end.

11 Now it's time to add the ties that will hold your seat pad in place.
    Start by cutting four pieces of ribbon, each 35 cm (13¾ inches).*

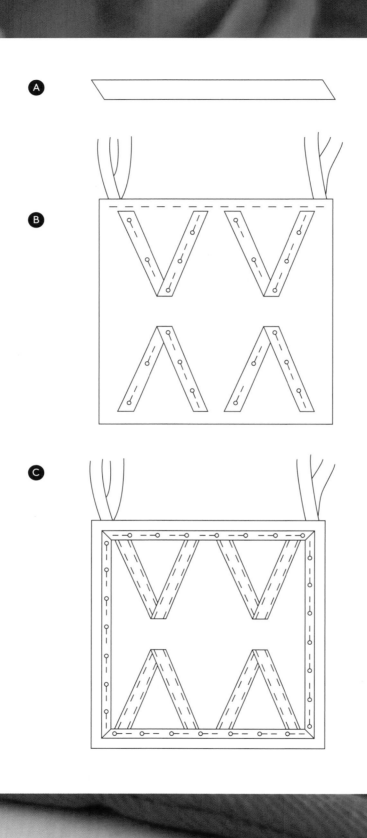

12 Hold two pieces of ribbon together, one on top of the other, and tuck these into the open edge 1.5 cm (inch) from the right-hand seam (tuck in roughly 3 cm (1 ¼ inches) of ribbon). Pin in place. Repeat on the left-hand side of the open edge with the other pieces of ribbon.

13 Now, starting 1.5 cm (⅝ inch) from one side and finishing 1.5 cm (⅝ inch) from the other, machine stitch along this edge, removing the pins as you go.

14 Next we need to make the ribbon pattern on the seat pad. Cut four lengths of ribbon, each about 30 cm (12 inches) long, with the ends cut at an angle, as in diagram A.

15 With the ribbon ties facing away from you, measure and mark with tailor's chalk the middle of the top and bottom edges of the pad (this will help you position your ribbon pattern).

16 Fold each of your pieces of ribbon to form a triangle 15 cm (6 inches) at its base and pin these to the seat pad, following the pattern shown in diagram B.

17 Removing the pins as you go, sew around the ribbon slightly in from the outer edge. Repeat, sewing slightly in from the inner edge.

18 Next, take a long strip of ribbon (about 160 cm [63 inches] long). Fold the end of the ribbon over to give a neat edge and place this square to one of the corners, 1.5 cm (⅝ inch) in from the edges. Pin the ribbon all the way around the seat pad (see diagram C), forming a 45-degree fold at each corner and covering the open ends of your ribbon triangles.

19 When you've reached all the way round, fold the end of the ribbon over to give a neat edge, and then fold at 45-degrees to form a neat corner. Pin in place.

20 Now sew your ribbon down in the same way as before, sewing along the outer and then the inner edges, removing the pins as you go.

21 Use the ribbon ties to secure your seat pad to the back uprights of your chair and sit comfortably!

* If your chairs have solid backs, use one longer ribbon tie on each side of the pad, making sure they are long enough to reach around the back of your chair and tie together.

MAKE IT YOUR OWN

- *If you're short on time or fancy a simpler look you could leave out the ribbon appliqué and simply stitch around the edge of your seat pad 1 cm (⅜ inch) in from the edge, then 3 cm (1 ¼ inches) in from the edge, and finally 5 cm (2 inches) in from the edge, to create a quilted look without the ribbon.*

- *For portable garden or picnic cushions, instead of attaching the ribbon ties, attach a small loop (about 20 cm [8 inches] of ribbon) at one corner only, so you can carry the cushions with ease!*

DECORATING

Here's where you really get to explore your personal taste and the styles you're drawn to. My favourite projects in this chapter are the wall hangings on pages 92 and 96. They are a fantastic (and cheap!) way to really assert the style of a particular space, to create a focus and add instant interest to a bare wall. The possibilities for making both of these projects your own are endless – play around with patterns, colours, textures and scale and see what you discover.

Similarly, making your own lampshades opens up so many possibilities for exploring design, whether it's a bold or a subtle statement you want to make.

Stencilled Wall Hanging

The pattern for this hanging was inspired by the small piece of hand-woven fabric at the beginning of this book (see page 7).
I really enjoy something about the visual relationship between the long, stretched triangles and the little short ones, so I thought I'd experiment with something similar here. I wanted to keep the colours neutral to subdue the bold pattern, but I couldn't resist adding a touch of subtle luxury by using white pearlescent ink.

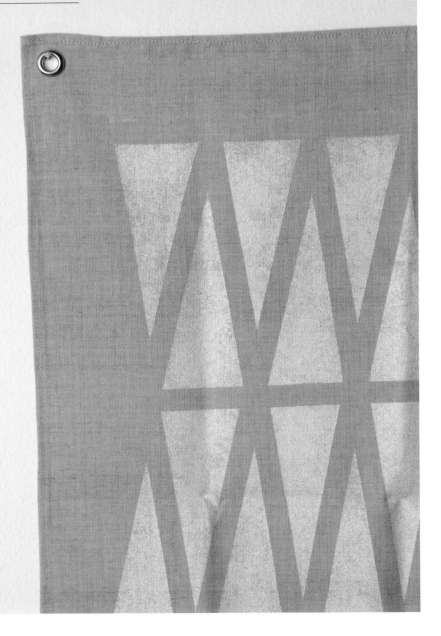

MATERIALS AND EQUIPMENT

M

- Mid-weight cotton fabric, at least 45 cm x 105 cm (17¾ inches x 41½ inches) (I've used an unbleached fair trade organic cotton)
- Permaset eco-friendly screen-printing ink in Metallic Pearl White
- Cotton thread to match your fabric
- Eyelet kit with two 1.5 cm (⅝ inch) silver eyelets

E

- Pencil
- Tape measure
- Scissors
- Old newspapers to protect your work surface
- Masking tape in two different widths: 1 cm (⅜ inch) and 2.4 cm (1 inch)
- Stencilling brush
- Pins
- Sewing machine
- Hammer and 2 small nails for hanging

MAKE IT YOUR OWN

- *Experiment with masking out other shapes and patterns, and use different colour combinations – from a simple grid in pale pastels to a complex geometric web in vivid brights.*

- *If stencilling isn't quite your thing, look again at some of the other projects in this book for inspiration – you could use machine appliqué, wool embroidery or even dip-dying for your wall hanging (see pages 120, 54 and 126).*

HOW TO

1 Cut your fabric to measure 45 cm x 105 cm (17¾ inches x 41⅜ inches).

2 On a hard, flat surface, spread out some old newspaper to protect against any ink seeping through your fabric when you start stencilling. Lay out your fabric (face up if it has a best side) on top of the newspaper. To keep your fabric in place, use a strip of masking tape across each corner to tape it to your surface.

3 To mask out your triangles, follow diagram A (or make up your own pattern). Once your pattern is masked out, press the masking tape down firmly to ensure crisp, clean edges.

4 Next, lightly dip the tip of your stencilling brush in the ink (don't overload the brush) and begin filling in the triangles you've masked out using a dabbing action. With stencilling, it's important to use a repeated dabbing motion, pressing the flat face of the brush straight down onto the fabric, rather than brushing from side to side. Continue until all your triangles are filled in, then leave to dry for a few hours or ideally overnight.

5 Once the ink is fully dry, peel away the masking tape. Now all you need to do is hem the edges and add the eyelets.

6 Turn your fabric over so the stencilled pattern is facing down. Working all the way around the fabric, fold in the edge by 0.5 cm (¼ inch) then fold over by another 0.5 cm (¼ inch) and pin in place.

7 Once you have pinned your hem securely, use your sewing machine to sew all the way round, 0.3 cm (⅛ inch) from the edge, removing the pins as you go.

8 Make a pencil mark in each of the top corners of your hanging, roughly 3 cm (1¼ inches) from the top and the sides, where your eyelets will go.

9 Eyelet kits vary, so follow the instructions for the one you have to insert the eyelets with the neater side (the side that doesn't get squished down) on the front of your hanging.

10 Now it's ready to hang. Hold your hanging in place and lightly mark through the eyelets with a pencil. Hammer small nails where you've marked and hang the eyelets over the nails.

A

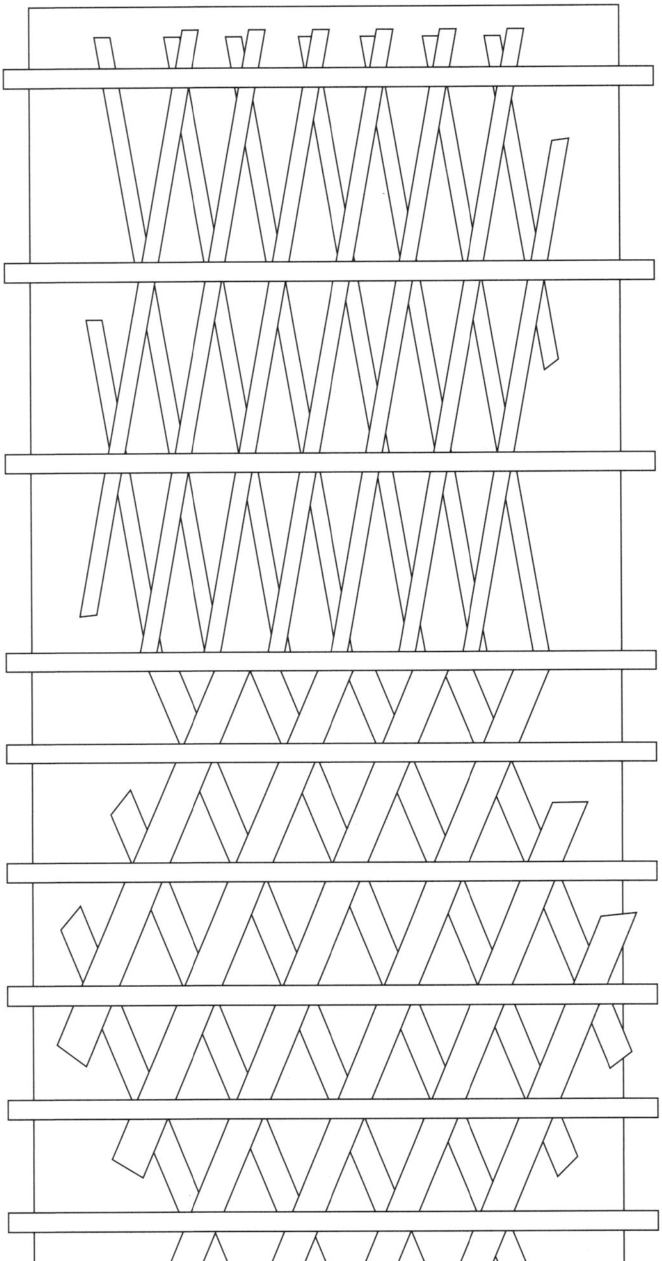

Knitted Wall Hanging

To use food as an analogy, this is one of those projects that's less like following a recipe and more like the kind of cooking where you balance out the flavours as you go, adding a bit more salt or a squeeze of lemon juice, until it's just right (that's my kind of cooking, and my kind of crafting too.). Once you've knitted your base, you can build up your 'rag-rug' sections bit by bit, creating just the right mix of colours and shapes. It's a time-consuming process but you'll end up with a stunning focal piece for your space.

MATERIALS AND EQUIPMENT

Don't worry if you've never knitted before, you can find lots of tutorials online teaching basic knitting stitches including how to cast on.

M
- Off-white chunky wool (I've used Cascade Ecological Undyed Peruvian Highland wool)
- Grey chunky wool (I've used an undyed Rowan Purelife British Sheep Breeds wool)
- 2 x 30 cm (12 inch) long wooden dowels, approximately 0.5 cm (¼ inch) thick
- Large scraps of fabric in a variety of colours (I've used a mix of plain and cross-weave cottons in shades ranging from warm red to mustard-yellow, with highlights of blue and white to add contrast)

E
- 8 mm knitting needles (US size 11)
- Pencil and paper to sketch your pattern (optional)
- Hammer and 2 small nails for hanging

HOW TO

1 Using your off-white wool, cast on 28 stitches.

2 Knit 65 rows.

3 Change over to your grey wool. To do this, cut your off-white wool a short length from where you finished knitting and tie it to your grey wool. Trim the knot (don't worry if the knot shows on the front of your knitting, as it'll be hidden later).

4 Now knit 22 rows in your grey wool.

5 Cut your wool a short length from the end of your row, loop it back through a stitch on the row below and knot it securely.

6 Rather than casting off as you would normally do, simply slip the stitches off the needle and onto one of your pieces of dowel.

7 Slide the second piece of dowel through the stitches along the bottom row of your knitting, so that you have one piece of dowel at the top and one at the bottom.

8 Now it's time to 'rag-rug' your hanging! *(Traditionally, this kind of 'rag-rugging' was done using hessian as a backing, poking small strips of fabric between the threads using a tool called a 'proddy'. For this somewhat less traditional project you can use one of your knitting needles as your proddy and the knitting acts as the backing.)* Begin by cutting some of your fabric scraps into approximately 1 cm (⅜ inch) wide strips and then cut those strips into roughly 4 cm (1½ inch) long mini-strips.

9 You might want to sketch out on a piece of paper a pattern of shapes and colours to follow. Simple blocks, stripes or triangles work best for this technique. I've used a multicoloured stripe across the join between the two colours of knitting, a pattern of blocks and stripes at the top and a more detailed pattern of triangles for the bottom section.

10 With your knitting face down, and starting at the join between your two coloured knitted panels, take one of your little strips of fabric and use the tip of a knitting needle to poke one end of it through to the front between two strands of wool. Now fold the other end of your strip over a strand of wool and poke it through to the front too. Check that both ends of your strip are roughly even in length on the front of your hanging.

11 Take your next strip of fabric and poke one end through the next hole along in the same way. Fold the other end over a strand of wool and poke it through to the front.

12 Repeat this process, building up your pattern, strip by strip (it's a slow process, but worth the work!). Make sure your strips of fabric are tightly packed together to give a full, fluffy look.

13 Once you're happy with your rag-rugged sections at the top and bottom of your hanging, we can start to add some fluffy detail to the plain knitting. Start by turning your hanging over so it is face up.

14 We'll begin with the fluffy triangle you can see at the centre of the hanging in the image opposite. Cut a length of off-white wool about 6 cm (2 ⅜ inches) long. Find the stitch closest to the centre of your hanging and tuck one end of the length of wool through that stitch, under one strand of wool and out again at the front (so both ends of your little piece of wool are sticking out of the front of your knitting). Tie the two ends of your wool in a knot on the front of your hanging and trim the ends to roughly 1.5 cm (⅝ inch) long.

15 Now cut another 6 cm (2 ⅜ inches) length of wool. From the little knot you just tied, count up two rows of knitting and out by one stitch to the right – at this point take the piece of wool you just cut and tie it through a stitch in the same way as you did with the first knot, then trim the ends to 1.5 cm (⅝ inch) long.

16 Repeat step 15 (moving up and out each time) until you reach the rag-rugged join. Then repeat on the left-hand side.

17 You should now have an upside down triangle of little knots! To turn this into a fluffy line, gently pull apart the strands of wool on each knot so they become fluffy.

18 Below your triangle, add two more fluffy lines in the same way, tying a knot on every other stitch along a row. You can vary the placement of your lines (or add more/fewer) to balance out the overall composition of your hanging.

19 Once you're happy with how it's looking, it's ready to hang! Hold the hanging in place and lightly mark just below the top dowel on each side, about 1.5 cm (⅝ inch) in from the ends. Hammer your small nails where you've marked and rest the dowel on the nails.

MAKE IT YOUR OWN

- Add other elements to the hanging, like pompoms along the bottom or tassels at the sides (see pages 73 and 105).

- If you're not a knitter, you could use a piece of hessian as the background (as most rag-rugs do) and rag-rug the whole surface.

- If you're a knitting superstar how about mixing rows of different stitches and colours to create a wall hanging that's all about the knitting?

Lampshades

This chapter is all about the finishing touches – the details that really make a space feel like it's your own. Lampshades are a great example of items that are functional but that have a whole lot of room for expressing your personal style. The lampshade kits that are now readily available (I buy mine online at www. needcraft.co.uk) make it so simple to experiment with colour, pattern, texture, size and shape. Plain or patterned fabrics work really well, but to give your lampshades even more bespoke style here are some ways of printing or embroidering your own fabric.

MATERIALS AND EQUIPMENT

M
- A lampshade kit (choose a size and shape to suit your space)
- Fabric (see the details in your particular kit for the exact dimensions of fabric you'll need and then make sure your fabric is at least 5 cm [2½ inches] larger than this in both directions)

E
- Scissors
- Tailor's chalk

For the geometric stencilled version you will also need:
- Permaset eco-friendly screen-printing ink
- Old newspapers to protect your work surface
- Masking tape
- Stencilling brush

For the machine-embroidered stripy version you will also need:
- Cotton thread in a range of colours
- Sewing machine

For the printed stripy version you will also need:
- Permaset eco-friendly screen-printing ink
- Old newspapers to protect your work surface
- Masking tape
- A hair comb
- An old plate or plastic lid bigger than your comb

Each lampshade kit comes with full instructions, so I won't repeat those here. It's definitely possible to make these lampshades on your own (I've done it!) but it is easier with a helper.

HOW TO

FOR THE MACHINE-EMBROIDERED STRIPY VERSION
This effect creates a really lovely texture on a plain fabric. Add subtle or bold colours depending on what level of contrast you'd like to achieve.

1   Make sure your rectangle of fabric is at least 5 cm (2 inches) larger in both directions than you need for your lampshade, as the zigzag stitch can cause the fabric to bunch up a little.

2   Set your sewing machine to a medium or large zigzag stitch and start sewing stripes across your fabric (from one long side to the other). You can measure out the stripes and mark them with tailor's chalk before starting if you want to be precise, or just sew freestyle if you don't mind a slightly more organic look. Leave strips of unsewn fabric at least 6 cm (2 ⅜ inches) wide between each group of stitched stripes (this will help your fabric stick to the backing when you make up your lampshade).

3   Change the colour of your thread and add more stripes. Continue in this way with as many different colours as you want, until you're happy with your fabric. Now you're ready to make your lampshade!

FOR THE GEOMETRIC STENCILLED VERSION

I've used a pale, pearlescent screen-printing ink on a dark navy cotton to create a bold pattern, but you could choose less contrasting colours for a more subtle look or use a lighter fabric to allow more light to come through.

1   On a hard, flat surface, spread out some old newspaper to protect against any ink seeping through your fabric when you start stencilling. Lay out your fabric (face up if it has a best side) on top of the newspaper. To keep your fabric in place, use a strip of masking tape across each corner to tape it to your surface.

2   Your lampshade kit will come with a rolled-up rectangle of sticky-backed plastic. Lay this out on top of your fabric leaving at least 2.5 cm (1 inch) of fabric around the edge, and draw around the plastic with your tailor's chalk. Set the plastic to one side for later.

3   Using masking tape, mask out a geometric pattern on your fabric (perhaps a series of simple stripes or a pattern of triangles?). Use the chalk outline as a guide if you want your pattern to work in a particular way around the shade (and note that the top and bottom 1 cm (⅜ inch) of the chalked rectangle will be tucked over the edge of the finished lamp).

4   Once your pattern is masked out, press the masking tape down firmly to ensure crisp, clean edges.

5   Next, lightly dip the tip of your stencilling brush in the ink (don't overload the brush) and begin filling in the pattern using a dabbing action. With stencilling, it's important to use a repeated dabbing motion, pressing the flat face of the brush straight down onto the fabric, rather than brushing from side to side. Once your pattern is complete, leave to dry for a few hours or overnight.

6   When the ink is dry, peel away the tape and your fabric is ready to use.

FOR THE PRINTED STRIPY VERSION

Using a hair comb as a printing tool may seem a little odd, but it's a really quick way to create a lovely, delicate pattern!

1   On a hard, flat surface, spread out some old newspaper to protect against any ink seeping through your fabric when you start printing. Lay out your fabric (face up if it has a best side) on top of the newspaper. To keep your fabric in place, use a strip of masking tape across each corner to tape it to your surface.

2   Pour a dollop of ink onto your plate or plastic lid. Dip the teeth of your comb into the ink and then press it firmly onto your fabric (the teeth should create a little row of dots). You might want to practise this on some scrap fabric first.

3   Repeat step 2 until you're happy with your pattern. I've printed lines parallel to the short edges of the fabric, so the pattern ends up as vertical stripes, but you could print at an angle or crisscross your lines for a more dynamic pattern.

MAKE IT YOUR OWN

•   *I often see vintage lamp bases minus their original shades, or with a shade that hasn't stood the test of time. Making your own lampshade for a vintage base can be an ideal way of giving it a new lease of life. You could match the vintage base with some vintage fabric or bring the base up to date with something more contemporary.*

•   *Lampshade kits come in a range of sizes, so think about playing with scale in different rooms and experiment with a pendant or table lamp.*

Wooden
Light
Pull

*This may seem like a small,
somewhat insignificant project
(compared to making your
own lampshades or a quilt)
but these little details around
your home can really make
it special and, most importantly,
feel like yours.*

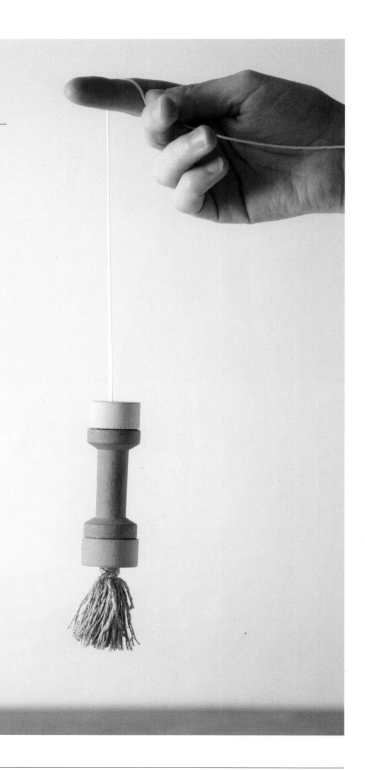

MATERIALS AND EQUIPMENT

I've used a wooden cotton reel from the organic cotton thread I use in my studio, and two smaller wooden reels from the middle of some vintage ribbon spools. You can find vintage reels and bobbins for sale on eBay or in vintage shops and markets, each with their own particular shape and character.

M

- Wooden cotton reels, ribbon reels or bobbins
- Eco-friendly acrylic paint
- Wood glue
- Wool (just enough to make one tassel, so a great way to use up leftovers)

E

- Small paintbrush
- Two pieces of card, each 6 cm (2⅜ inches) x 6 cm (2⅜ inches)
- Scissors
- Pencil

MAKE IT YOUR OWN

- If a simpler, more minimal look would suit your décor better, use large wooden beads instead of cotton reels and leave them unpainted or apply a varnish or stain to the wood.

- The technique used in the Striped Clothes Pegs project (see page 26) would be a perfect way to add a geometric pattern.

HOW TO

1   Make sure your reels and bobbins are clean and ready to paint. I've chosen a different colour for each one, but you can vary this to suit your décor.

2   Paint all the faces of your reels and bobbins, allowing one side to dry before turning over to paint the other side. Apply 3 or 4 coats of paint until you have a smooth, even finish.

3   Once your reels are painted and completely dry, decide what order to stack them in to create the best shape. Glue your stack together by applying glue to the faces of the reels and pressing them together gently, wiping away any excess glue. Make sure the holes in the centre of each reel align with one another. Leave to dry.

4   Next, make your tassel! Take your two pieces of card and wrap wool around them until you have enough for a nice bushy tassel. Now snip between the two pieces of card, along the bottom of the wool. Carefully slide the wool off the card, keeping it all together in a little bundle.

5   Slide a pencil through the top of the wool loops. Take a piece of wool about 20 cm (8 inches) long and tie this tightly around the wool tassel, just below the pencil. Wrap the piece of wool round and round the tassel, then tie in a double knot and trim the ends. This wrapped section needs to be quite a bit thicker than the hole in the bottom of your reel stack, so that the tassel doesn't slide through! Remove the pencil.

6   Now you're ready to attach everything to your light pull-cord. Thread the light pull-cord through your reel stack, from top to bottom. Thread the end of the cord through the loop on the tassel (where the pencil was) and tie a knot above the tassel. Spread some glue over the top of your tassel, just above the wrapped section. Tuck the knot up into the bottom of the reel stack and pull the reel stack down to cover the knot and the loop. Wipe away any excess glue and leave to dry for a few hours before using.

Painted Plant-pot Holders

I love it when something functional (like a plant-pot holder) doubles up as a design feature adding a bold dose of colour. I'm a complete plant addict (as the unfeasible number of plants that grace our small flat and 'balcony garden' attest to). This incredibly simple project will transform a cluster of random houseplants into a real feature.

MATERIALS AND EQUIPMENT

I've suggested using clear glass bowls and glasses so that you only need to paint the outside, as the colour will show through to the inside. You can use ceramic bowls instead, but you'll probably need to paint the inside as well to cover up any pattern or colour, and the paint may not stand up well to being regularly soaked when you water your plants (not so bad for cacti though!).

The glasses and bowls I've used were picked up from my local charity shop for 20p each!

M
- Vintage clear glass bowls or glasses big enough for your plant pots to sit in (I think a collection of at least 4 or 5 in different sizes and shapes looks great)
- Eco-friendly acrylic paint

E
- Old newspapers to protect your work surface
- Tins of beans (or something similar!) to hold up your drying bowls or glasses (the tin should fit inside the bowl or glass)
- Medium paintbrush
- Small paintbrush

HOW TO

1   Thoroughly wash and dry your bowls or glasses.

2   Spread out some old newspaper and then set out your tins ready to sit each bowl or glass on upside down, so that they can dry without sticking to anything.

3   Take your first bowl or glass and paint the whole of the outside and the bottom. Be careful to paint the top rim neatly (I find it easier to do this area with a smaller brush).

4   Sit your painted bowl or glass upside down over one of your tins and leave it to dry. Don't worry if the paint looks quite streaky at this point, it will even out as you build up the coats.

5   Repeat with the rest of your bowls or glasses and leave them to dry completely (be sure to rinse out your brushes between each coat, as acrylic paint dries quickly).

6   Once your first coat of paint has dried, apply another coat and allow to dry. Repeat, until you have a good solid colour and no visible streaks (this may take 4 or 5 coats of paint).

7   Once you're happy with your plant-pot holders and they're completely dry, add your plants (still in their pots) and arrange them on a windowsill or anywhere with plenty of sunlight.

MAKE IT YOUR OWN

- *For a vintage feel, you could simply use a collection of pretty vintage crockery, leaving them just as they are (but watch out for any cracks that might leak water!). You can be as random as you like, or you could collect pieces that all feature a particular colour or pattern.*

- *I've suggested painting these plant-pot holders all the same colour, but it would look really striking to paint one a completely different colour, or to paint each one its own unique shade.*

Plaited Mat

I love how rugs and mats add colour, texture and warmth to a space, all while being practical! This little mat gives such a welcoming pop of zigzag stripes to any doorway. You could easily scale it up to make a small rug or runner for a hallway.

MATERIALS AND EQUIPMENT

The exact amount of fabric you'll need to make the plaits will depend on the weight of the fabric and how tightly you plait it. Make your plaits in stages so you don't use up more fabric than you need. This is a great way to use up pieces of fabric left over from other projects.

M

- Neutral-coloured plain heavyweight cotton fabric for the backing, at least 50 cm x 70 cm (20 inches x 27½ inches) (I've used a heavy fair trade texweave cotton)
- Cotton thread to complement your fabric colours
- 2–3 m (2⅛ – 3¼ yards) light- or mid-weight fabric (I've used organic cotton cross-weave fabric in shades of blue, orange and dark plum)

E

- Tailor's chalk
- Tape measure
- Scissors
- Pins
- Sewing machine

MAKE IT YOUR OWN

- To make a more traditional circular rag-rug you can simply zigzag stitch your plaits together in a coil, working out from the centre (with no need for a backing fabric).

- This technique is perfect for making trivets for your kitchen or placemats for the dining table (just make sure you use heat-resistant fabrics).

HOW TO

1 Measure and cut out a 50 x 70 cm (19¾ x 27⅝ inches) rectangle from your backing fabric.

2 With the right side of the fabric facing down, fold over the edge 5 cm (2 inches) all the way around, pinning it in place.

3 Machine stitch to secure and then set the backing aside.

4 Start cutting your pieces of fabric into long strips, about 3 cm (1¼ inches) wide (I do this just a few at a time, so I don't end up with more strips than I need and I can decide on the colours as I go along).

5 Take three strips of the same colour and stitch them together at one end. Plait them, and then stitch the other ends together to secure. Repeat with a few more strips, so you have a handful of long plaits.

6 Place your backing fabric face down on a flat surface, so that the hemmed edge is showing. Take your first plait and fold one end under about 2 cm (¾ inch), to conceal the untidy finish and stitching. Keeping the end folded under, pin the plait across the middle of your backing fabric in a zigzag pattern. When you get to the other side, cut off any excess plait leaving 2 cm (¾ inch) extending past the edge of the backing. Tuck this end under, hiding it between the plait and the backing. Make sure your plait overhangs a little at either side so that the backing is concealed.

7 Save the lengths of excess plait you cut off for later.

8 Repeat the process with the next plait, lining it up as closely as possible along the edge of the first plait.

9 Set your sewing machine to a wide zigzag stitch and sew along the join between the two plaits (removing the pins as you go), securing them to each other and to the backing.

10 Pin another plait in place, again keeping it as close as possible to the previous one, and stitch together in the same way.

11 Continue in this way, working in both directions away from your first plait and varying your plait colours to create a stripy pattern.

12 When you've finished the last zigzags (which probably look more like wavy lines) along the top and bottom edges, use the off-cuts of plait to fill in the gaps and to complete the rectangle (as always, tucking in the loose ends before you sew them in place).

CELEBRATING

For me, celebrating should be an integral part of any home – whether it's throwing a party, toasting a big or small success, or just marking the end of a difficult week! It's always worth stepping out of the day-to-day to celebrate something. It doesn't take much to add a feeling of celebration to a familiar space – coloured garlands, a fancy tablecloth or just some bespoke candle holders will do it (see pages 118, 120 and 130 for inspiration). And, if it's sunny, there's little more celebratory than a picnic! Add some style and comfort to your outdoor feast with the Picnic Blanket project on page 134 – and maybe bring along some cushions or seat pads from Chapter 2!

Tassels
Garland

Alongside cake, I think garlands
are one of the best ways to create
an instant sense of celebration
and occasion. And once the party's
over you don't necessarily have
to pack them away: as a more
permanent fixture, draped
over a mirror or across a window
or bookcase, they're a lovely
way to add colour and movement
to a space.

MATERIALS AND EQUIPMENT

M

- Light- or mid-weight fabric, at least 60 x 10 cm (23 ⅝ inches x 4 inches) for each tassel (this is a great way to use up larger scraps. I've used a mix of fair trade organic cottons and peace silk)
- String, however long you want your garland to be

E

- Scissors
- 2 squares of stiff card, measuring 15 cm x 15 cm (6 inches x 6 inches)

MAKE IT YOUR OWN

- *The tassel options are endless: you can vary the length, colours and fabrics of your tassels, or don't use fabric at all, try tissue paper, ribbon, wool …*

- *Once you've mastered tassels, why not branch out into pompom garlands, or strings of fabric lace flags (see pages 73 and 130).*

HOW TO

1 Choose your first piece of fabric and cut it into long, thin strips approximately 0.5–0.8 cm (¼ inch) wide.

2 Hold the two squares of card face to face with the string sandwiched between them, running from left to right.

3 Begin wrapping one of your fabric strips around the middle of the card from the bottom to the top. Keep wrapping more strips of fabric around the card until you're happy with the fullness of your tassel.

4 Cut one long, thin strip of fabric in a contrasting colour and set aside.

5 Pull the string on either side of the card up until it reaches the top.

6 At the bottom, slide your scissors between the two sheets of card and cut across the strips of fabric.

7 Carefully remove the sheets of card, bunching together your strips of fabric to make a nice full tassel.

8 Take the contrasting strip of fabric you cut in step 4 and tie it tightly around your tassel, just below the string.

9 Wrap the ends of the strip firmly around the tassel in opposite directions to form a 2 cm (¾ inch) binding. Tie the ends in a double knot and trim off any excess fabric.

10 Trim off any uneven ends from the bottom of your tassel.

11 Repeat steps 1 to 10 using up your remaining fabrics to make as many tassels as your garland needs. Be sure to space your tassels evenly along the string.

12 When you've finished all your tassels, tie a loop at each end of your string, and you're ready to hang it up.

Machine-
appliqué
Tablecloth

This little tablecloth is perfect for a
small kitchen or patio table, but you
could easily scale it up to dress a
larger dining table by either using
a larger piece of fabric or using
a plain tablecloth and laying this
one across the centre like a runner.

MATERIALS AND EQUIPMENT

M
- Mid-weight cotton fabric, 100 cm x 120 cm (39½ inches x 47¼ inches), or to fit your table (I've used fair trade organic cotton in a very pale blue)
- Cotton thread in the same colour as your main fabric
- 4 m (4⅜ yards) ribbon approximately 2.5 cm (1 inch) wide in a contrasting colour (I've used a deep red vintage ribbon)
- Roughly 25 cm x 50 cm (10 inches x 20 inches) fabric in a similar colour to your ribbon, for the appliqué (I've used scraps of deep red fine corduroy)
- Cotton thread in the same colour as your appliqué fabric

E
- Scissors
- Tape measure
- Pins
- Sewing machine
- Tailor's chalk
- Iron

MAKE IT YOUR OWN

- *For a really simple, everyday tablecloth you could simply hem your fabric and then appliqué on a strip of patterned ribbon (or lace) all the way around, a little way in from the edges (machine stitch along both edges of your ribbon or lace). Check the washing instructions of your trim first if you want to throw your tablecloth in the washing machine!*

- *Hand embroidery is another great way to decorate a tablecloth! Don't be daunted by the expanse of fabric – you can just focus on the edges that you'll see hanging over the sides of your table. See the Wool-embroidered Cushion project on page 54 for inspiration.*

HOW TO

1   Make sure your fabric is a neat rectangle (or cut to your preferred size).

2   With the right side of the fabric facing down, fold over the edge 1 cm (⅜ inch) then fold it over again by another 1 cm (⅜ inch) all the way around, pinning in place.

3   Machine stitch 0.5 cm (¼ inch) from the edge to secure the hem, removing the pins as you go.

4   Once your tablecloth is hemmed, give it a press with an iron and lay it out face up on a flat surface (I usually do this on the floor).

5   Next we need to create a ribbon bow in each corner. Follow diagram A to create your bows, pinning them in place (see the photo on page 123 for how to position your bows).

6   Use your sewing machine to stitch the bows in place using matching coloured thread. Straight stitch along both edges of the ribbon so it is flat against the tablecloth.

7   Now we can add the appliqué flowers and leaves. You can trace or copy the templates on page 124, or make up your own. Either way, draw your flowers and leaves onto your other piece of fabric with tailor's chalk. Cut them out carefully and pin them to your tablecloth, right side facing up, to create your pattern.

8   Once you are happy with the placement of your flowers and leaves, use a zigzag stitch around their edges and remove the pins. Now your tablecloth is ready for your next celebration!

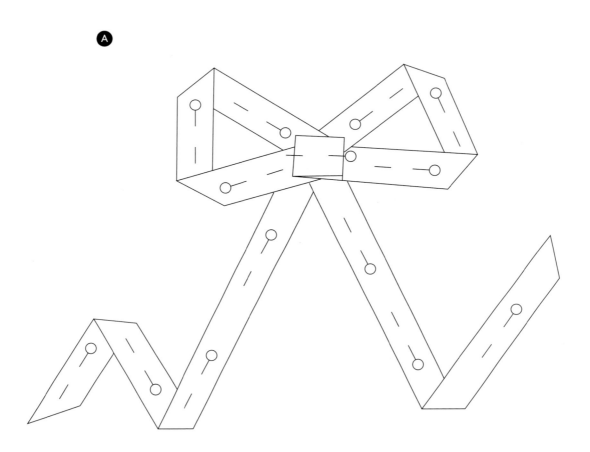

Template

Dip-dyed Ribbon

I usually make a whole batch of these, as it's such a quick and easy process. Then I have pretty ribbon ready for wrapping gifts, tying flowers, decorating jars and vases, and using in all sorts of sewing projects.

MATERIALS AND EQUIPMENT

M
- Permaset eco-friendly screen-printing inks
- Lengths of ribbon (I've used a selection of off-white vintage and new ribbons of varying widths and lengths. Different colours and materials will absorb the dye in different ways, producing a range of results – which is, of course, half the excitement of making something yourself.)

E
- Small paintbrush
- Small glass or plastic bowl
- Drying rack or clothes rack to dry your ribbons
- Old newspapers to protect your floor from drips.

MAKE IT YOUR OWN

- *For a celebratory meal or a picnic these would look stunning tied in bows around sets of cutlery.*

- *You don't have to use white ribbon – any pale colour will work. The ribbon colour will affect how the colour of the dye shows up though, so experiment with different combinations.*

HOW TO

1. Use the paintbrush to add about a teaspoonful of the screen-printing ink to your bowl. Top it up with water to a depth of about 2.5cm (1 inch). Mix well with your paintbrush (I quite like leaving a few small lumps of ink unmixed so that the dye is uneven and has some stronger blotches).

2. Take your first piece of ribbon* and fold in half, so the two ends meet. Submerge the ends into your watery ink as far up as you want the dye to reach. Pull the ribbon slowly from the ink, squeezing it between your fingers so as to remove as much liquid as possible (do this over the bowl so you can re-use the ink).

3. For a stronger colour, repeat the dipping process. You could also dip less of the ribbon the second time, so the colour is stronger towards the ends.

4. Once you are happy with your ribbon, lay it out, unfolded, over the drying rack to dry. Be sure to place newspaper on the surface underneath your ribbon to catch any drips of dye.

5. Repeat the process with your other ribbons, using other ink colours. Leave all your ribbons to dry.

6. Once your ribbons are completely dry, give them an iron to help set the colour and to remove any creases.

   For a crisper edge to your dyed area, start with a dry ribbon. If you would like a softer look, wet your ribbon before dying – experiment to get the look you want.

Fabric
Lace
Candle
Jars

Candles are definitely on my list of celebration essentials and while old jam jars with tea lights are beautiful just as they are, this quick project makes them just a little more celebratory. Making the 'fabric lace' for this project works on the same principle as making paper snowflakes and is quite addictive!

MATERIALS AND EQUIPMENT

M

- Clean, empty jam jars
- Scraps of light- to mid-weight fabric in your choice of colours (see step 1 to find our how big your scraps need to be)
- Tea lights (one for each of your jars)
- Double-sided tape

E

- Tape measure
- Sharp scissors
- Iron

MAKE IT YOUR OWN

- For an even quicker version you could use scraps of vintage lace instead of making the fabric lace. Vintage glasses also work really well in place of jam jars.

- These pretty glass jars also look lovely filled with fresh flowers.

- You can put fabric lace to lots of other uses, from a Mexican-style banner garland (with rectangles of fabric lace sewn along a length of ribbon) to quick and striking table decorations (use large circles of fabric lace as place settings and scatter the cut-out scraps over the table like confetti!).

HOW TO

1 Measure around the outside of your jar, then add 1.5 cm (⅝ inch). This will be the length of fabric you need for decorating that jar. Now measure the height of your jar and take 3 cm (1¼ inch) off the measurement. This will be the width of fabric you'll need.

2 Repeat this for all your jars if they are different sizes and cut out a rectangle of fabric to fit each one.

3 Take one of your pieces of fabric and fold over one of its shorter edges 2 cm (¾ inch). Continue to fold all the way along the fabric, back and forth, like a concertina.

4 Now it's time to snip out your pattern along the edges (you can go freestyle or use diagram A for guidance).

5 Unfold your fabric and give it a quick press with an iron.

6 Cut a strip of double-sided tape the same length as the short edge of your fabric and stick the tape vertically on the side of your jar.

7 Cut some smaller pieces of double-sided tape and stick these on the reverse of the fabric along one of the short edges, avoiding any holes you've cut.

8 With the right side of the fabric now facing you, press the other short edge (the one without tape) along the tape on the jar. Wrap the fabric all the way around the jar and press down the sticky-taped end where your fabric overlaps.

9 Repeat steps 3 to 8 for each of your jars and then add a candle to each jar.

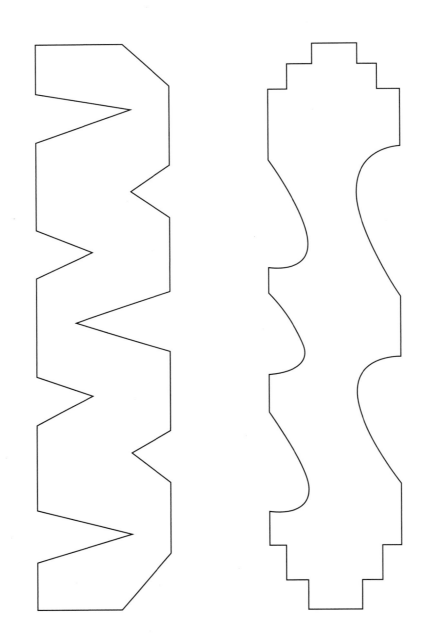

Picnic
Blanket

I love a picnic! Whether it's on a beach, in the park or just on my balcony, I always feel like there's something special about eating outdoors, especially in England, where the opportunity comes so rarely!

MATERIALS AND EQUIPMENT

M

You'll need fabrics that are heavy enough to provide a bit of padding and that can withstand some wear and tear. For the main fabric I found a gorgeous piece of vintage checked wool tweed that was crying out for a new life as a picnic blanket!

- Vintage checked wool tweed (or a similar soft but tough fabric), at least 200 cm x 120 cm (79 inches x 47¼ inches)
- Cotton thread to suit your fabric
- Neutral-coloured heavyweight cotton fabric, at least 150 cm x 120 cm (59 inches x 47¼ inches) (I've used a fair trade texweave)

E

- Tape measure
- Scissors
- Iron
- Pins
- Sewing machine
- Pencil
- Tailor's chalk

HOW TO

1   We'll start by making the ties that will go around your blanket. Cut two strips of fabric, each 20 cm (8 inches) wide, from one of the shorter edges of your main fabric.

2   Lay one of your strips of fabric on a flat surface, right side facing down. Fold over one end about 1 cm (⅜ inch) and press the fold with an iron so it stays in place.

3   Next fold over the long sides of your strip so that they meet in the middle. Press in place with the iron (and make sure the end is still folded in).

4   Now fold the strip over lengthways, so that the two long edges meet. Press with an iron and pin in place (your strip should now be roughly 5 cm [2 inches] wide).

5   Machine stitch all the way around the edges of your folded strip of fabric about 0.5 cm (¼ inch) in from the edge, removing the pins as you go.

6   Repeat steps 2 to 5 with the second strip.

7   Now we can move on to making the blanket itself. Measure and cut your main fabric to 150 cm x 120 cm (59¼ inches x 47¼ inches).

8   Measure and cut your backing fabric to the same size.

9   Lay out your backing fabric on a flat surface, right side facing up. Lay your main fabric on top, right side facing down, and line up the layers so that all the edges meet neatly.

10   Pin along each side, about 1 cm (⅜ inch) from the edge. Starting with a longer side, machine stitch around three of the sides, leaving one of the shorter edges open. Remove all the pins.

11   To give your blanket neater corners, cut across each one, a little way from the corners of your stitching (see the diagram on page 9).

12   Turn your blanket inside out and gently poke out the corners from the inside with a pencil (be careful not to poke too hard!). Give your blanket a press with an iron.

13 Along the open edge, fold in 2 cm (¾ inch) of backing fabric all the way along the bottom edge. Then fold in 2 cm (¾ inch) of the main fabric along the top edge. Pin in place about 1 cm (⅜ inch) from the edge, so the two edges are neatly lined up.

14 Measure and mark the middle of the open edge with your tailor's chalk. Take the two ties you made earlier and tuck the rough ends 2 cm (¾ inch) in to the open edge of your blanket on either side of the centre mark. Pin them in place.

15 To finish your blanket, sew along the open edge, 0.5 cm (¼ inch) from the edge, securing the ties in place. Continue stitching along the other sides of the blanket, always keeping 0.5 cm (¼ inch) from the edge. When you reach the folded edge again overlap the stitching by 1 cm (⅜ inch) or so to secure the ends.

16 Finally, roll up your blanket! With the ties facing away from you, fold the right and left sides of the blanket in to meet in the middle. Roll the blanket away from you until you reach the ties, then wrap one tie away from you and one towards you twice round the blanket, and tie in a bow.

MAKE IT YOUR OWN

- *I love the idea of this as a unique, romantic wedding present with the names of the couple embroidered in one corner of the fabric.*

- *For a thoroughly stylish (and, most importantly, comfortable) picnic, you could make a full picnic set with cushions and quilted blankets in colours to complement your picnic blanket.*

- *Luckily the piece of vintage fabric I found was large enough to make a whole picnic blanket, but if you have several smaller pieces, sew them together for a patchwork version.*

SUPPLIERS LIST

Sourcing your materials
Here's a list of some of the suppliers I buy materials from. Many of them focus on eco-ethical or British made products.

Cushion inserts:
  WoolSoft www.woolsoft.co.uk

Eco-friendly acrylic paints:
  Eco Green Crafts makes a range of eco-friendly acrylics which you can buy on
  www.amazonco.uk or in many online craft stores

Eco-friendly screen-printing inks:
  Permaset Screen printing inks www.permaset.co.uk (available in craft stores and online at
  www.amazon.co.uk or www.ebay.co.uk

Eco-friendly interiors paints and wood glue:
  Ecos Organic Paints www.ecosorganicpaints.co.uk

Lampshade kits:
  Need Craft www.needcraft.co.uk

Organic/Fairtrade fabrics:
  Organic Fabrics www.organiccotton.biz/store
  Offset Warehouse www.offsetwarehouse.com

Recycled Felt:
  The Felted Rainbow www.folksy.com/shops/thefeltedrainbow

Wool:
  Debbie Bliss (I use the eco baby and eco aran ranges) www.debbieblissonline.com
  Loop, London (stocks some lovely organic and undyed wool ranges) www.loopknittingshop.com

Vintage/second-hand fabrics:
  eBay www.ebay.co.uk
  Etsy www.etsy.com

ANNA ALICIA is the designer-maker behind jewellery and homeware label A Alicia. Over the past five years A Alicia has developed a reputation for producing contemporary and beautifully handcrafted ethical-textile jewellery and homeware. Ethical and environmental concerns are central to Anna Alicia, as is promoting the value of handcrafted products.

Anna Alicia took a roundabout route to design, via a degree in Art History at the University of Kent and an MA in Fine Art at Central Saint Martins in London. Her background in Art History and Fine Art plays a huge role in inspiring her collections, as do the travels of her childhood and the buzz of living and working in East London.

ACKNOWLEDGEMENTS

Thank you Stuart for the love and support.

Thank you Rachel for being like family.

Thank you Ayesha and Brian for thinking up great questions and for being the loveliest of people.

Thank you Grandad for giving me a love of learning and of going places.

Thank you to everyone who has worked on this book, especially Kate Pollard for asking me to do this and for always getting it, and Jacqui Melville for the beautiful photographs.

Thank you to all my friends for being exactly the beautiful, inspirational people you are.

www.aalicia.bigcartel.com

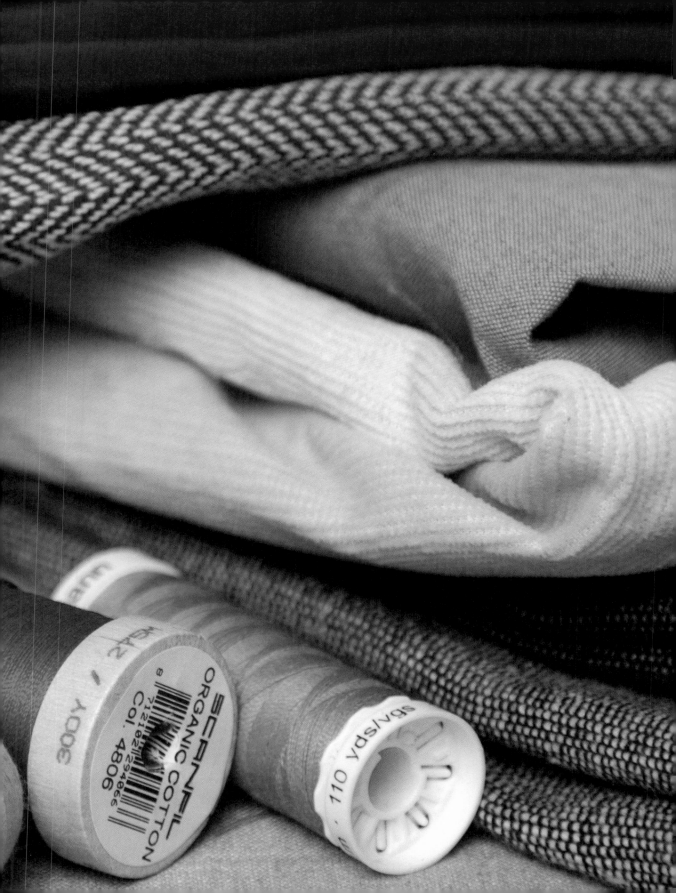

Make It Your Own by Anna Alicia

First published in 2013 by Hardie Grant Books

Hardie Grant Books (UK)
Dudley House, North Suite
34–35 Southampton Street
London WC2E 7HF
www.hardiegrant.co.uk

Hardie Grant Books (Australia)
Ground Floor, Building 1
658 Church Street
Melbourne, VIC 3121
www.hardiegrant.com.au

British Library Cataloguing-in-Publication Data. A catalogue record
for this book is available from the British Library.

ISBN 978-1-74270-599-6

Commissioning Editor: Kate Pollard
Desk Editor: Kajal Mistry
Photography: Jacqui Melville
Design: Charlotte Heal
Colour Reproduction by p2d

Printed and bound in China by 1010 Printing International Limited

10 9 8 7 6 5 4 3 2 1